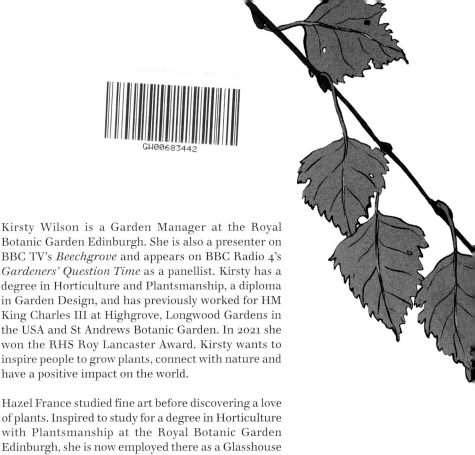

Kirsty Wilson is a Garden Manager at the Royal Botanic Garden Edinburgh. She is also a presenter on BBC TV's *Beechgrove* and appears on BBC Radio 4's *Gardeners' Question Time* as a panellist. Kirsty has a degree in Horticulture and Plantsmanship, a diploma in Garden Design, and has previously worked for HM King Charles III at Highgrove, Longwood Gardens in the USA and St Andrews Botanic Garden. In 2021 she won the RHS Roy Lancaster Award. Kirsty wants to inspire people to grow plants, connect with nature and have a positive impact on the world.

Hazel France studied fine art before discovering a love of plants. Inspired to study for a degree in Horticulture with Plantsmanship at the Royal Botanic Garden Edinburgh, she is now employed there as a Glasshouse Horticulturist, helping to conserve plants in the tropical collections. In her work as an illustrator, she is passionate about drawing plants as a way of capturing the liveliness, vibrance and detail of the natural world.

KIRSTY WILSON
ILLUSTRATED BY HAZEL FRANCE

Planting
with
Nature

A GUIDE TO
SUSTAINABLE
GARDENING

Royal
Botanic Garden
Edinburgh

BIRLINN

First published in 2023 by
Birlinn Limited
West Newington House
10 Newington Road
Edinburgh
EH9 1QS

birlinn.co.uk

and the Royal Botanic Garden Edinburgh

rbge.org.uk

ISBN: 978 1 78027 804 9

British Library Cataloguing-in-Publication Data
A catalogue record for this book is available
from the British Library

Designed and typeset by Mark Blackadder

Printed and bound by PNB, Latvia

Contents

Digitalis purpurea
(foxglove)

Foreword

Why wouldn't you want to attract wildlife to your garden? Whilst you would wish to draw the line at voracious herbivores such as rabbits, hares or deer, gardening with nature is a great way of adding colour, movement and interest, and achieving even more satisfaction from your horticultural labours. Encouraging wildlife into your garden can work in wonderful harmony with designing and maintaining your green space. It makes a meaningful, and much needed, contribution to the conservation of nature and improves the quality and health of our environment.

At the Royal Botanic Garden Edinburgh's four Gardens we encourage and take much joy from the native wildlife which flourish alongside 13,500 plant species in our care. From robins to red squirrels and beetles to butterflies, our Gardens provide a haven for over 1,000 indigenous species.

Parks and private gardens have much potential to sustain and develop urban biodiversity. According to the Office for National Statistics, the urban areas in the UK cover nearly two million hectares, the human occupants of which need nature for their health and wellbeing.

This stimulating book by Kirsty Wilson, beautifully illustrated by Hazel France, provides a wealth of information and tips for gardening for nature, and how to help nature play its part in creating a more sustainable and ecologically valuable garden. Whatever the size of your garden, *Planting with Nature* provides both the inspiration and expertise to live in closer harmony with the natural world and to get even more pleasure from your personal green space.

Simon Milne MBE FRSE FRGS
Regius Keeper
The Royal Botanic Garden Edinburgh

CHAPTER 1

The Living Garden

'To plant a garden is to believe in tomorrow'
AUDREY HEPBURN

As a child, I was always out in the Scottish countryside, and I loved observing the interactions of plants, insects, birds and other animals. The way that everything is interlinked fascinated me and as I have grown older, I have become more aware that humans and our actions are deeply connected to nature and the well-being of the planet. The natural world is made up of complex life cycles and food chains that have evolved over thousands of years. Sadly, our focus has tended to be on seeing the Earth as simply a provider of resources in terms of energy, building materials, food and consumables. As a result, forests have been destroyed, land has been over-cultivated, hedges have been removed, areas have been quarried, drained or concreted over and waste materials have been dumped. In addition, global warming as a result of increased carbon dioxide emissions from transport, heating and industry is also impacting on the balance of nature and the health of our planet for future generations. This can mean that certain birds, mammals and plant species are under threat, and they may become less visible in our gardens. Climate change may allow us to grow different plants in Scotland, but these exotic plants from other countries may not always benefit our local native wildlife.

Even in our own gardens, we have been actively encouraged to manicure our lawns and neatly clip our shrubs to produce something that is aesthetically pleasing. It is also not unknown for gardeners to use chemicals to fertilise and control so-called garden pests. However, a garden is a microcosm of the wider natural world, and our over-controlling behaviour is having a damaging effect on biodiversity and the overall health of the planet. In writing this book, I want to show that no matter the size of your garden, you can make a positive difference to support nature and biodiversity by making small changes to the way you manage and enjoy your gardening. If every household adopted just one idea from this book, we could make a big impact on the natural world. Your garden could safeguard many species like bees, butterflies, hedgehogs, birds, frogs, insects and a variety of plants as well as providing a beautiful space for you to enjoy. After all, we are all an integral part of the planet's nature and being in a biodiverse greenspace can make us happier, healthier and reduce our stress levels.

This book is about gardening with nature, a form of gardening where the emphasis is on us stepping back and letting nature play its role in our gardens in comparison to more active forms of garden management and control. There has been significant interest in sustainability with large-scale rewilding projects in the Highlands of Scotland, in north-east

Portugal, in Alaska, in the Danube delta and in many marine conservation areas around the world. These projects have been aimed at reversing the impact of humans and allowing the natural landscape and all the species that depend on it to recover. Many of the rewilding principles behind these large-scale projects can be adopted and adapted for our own gardens.

Some of the major rewilding projects have involved no intervention, letting nature take over, reversing humanity's activities and allowing the natural landscape to recover. However, as many of us live in towns and cities, a totally wild garden is unlikely to be very attractive to our neighbours or as a relaxing place to enjoy. Also, rabbits digging up your vegetables may not be one of the natural activities you really want to witness. It is more about creating a well-balanced sustainable garden where we can live in harmony with nature

Erica cinerea
(bell heather)

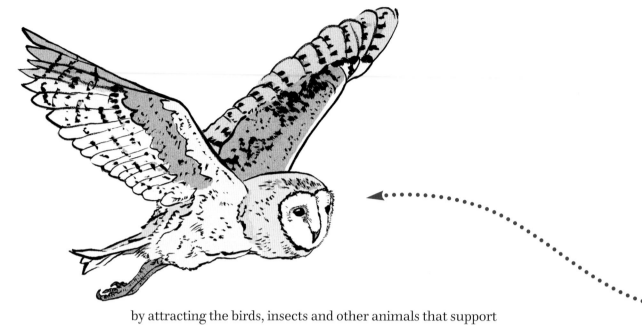

by attracting the birds, insects and other animals that support an effective garden ecosystem and undertaking garden tasks in such a way that we do not damage the planet.

It is important that we understand the interrelated nature of our garden ecosystem. If you start with trees and shrubs, they produce leaf mould and organic matter. This provides energy for primary consumers such as fungi and bacteria. Secondary consumers such as protozoa, nematodes and mites feed on these before being eaten by higher level consumers such as earthworms, beetles, spiders, centipedes and ants. These are a source of nourishment for birds, moles, and shrews which are then predated by larger mammals and birds. Introducing chemicals into our gardens or removing organic matter can break that chain. This may mean we have a soil with no worms to improve soil structure and water infiltration. There may be no ladybirds or house sparrows around to eat the aphids that have set up home on our roses. Our garden should not be a sterile area managed purely for aesthetics, but it should be teeming with all aspects of wildlife from fungi to insects and other animals. We need to allow nature to come into our gardens and trust that in time even with more pests, more predators will appear to control them, and the natural ecosystem will operate in a

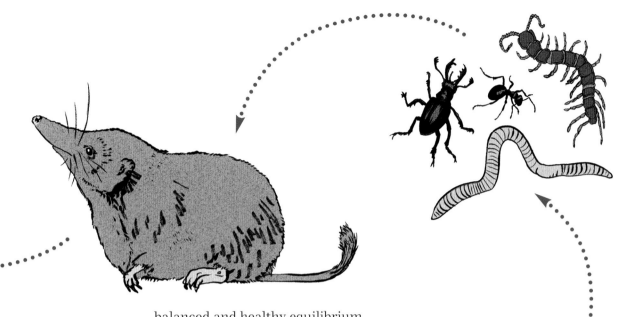

balanced and healthy equilibrium.

It is not just about insect and other animal species; it is also about plant species. Often plants that are frequently labelled as weeds are actually native flora that attract beneficial insects and birds into our gardens. For example, a small nettle patch can overwinter insects which provide early food for ladybirds, hedgehogs, shrews, frogs and toads. All of these are important for eating the garden 'pests' such as aphids, slugs and snails. Nettles also attract some of the country's most colourful and best-known butter-flies, such as the small tortoiseshell and peacock butterflies. Nothing brings a garden to life as much as watch-ing these butterflies dart around the flowers. I am not suggesting we dig up our flower beds and give them over to

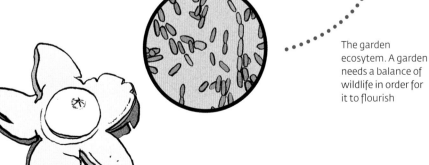

The garden ecosytem. A garden needs a balance of wildlife in order for it to flourish

Urtica dioica
(common stinging
nettle)

a bed of nettles, but a small patch of nettles in a corner or behind a shed can just provide that boost for biodiversity. Some wildflowers or even clover in the lawn can also attract many important pollinators such as bees.

Gardening for nature is also about the landscaping of our gardens. Hard landscaping with concrete or tarmac in driveways and patios can lead to waterlogging of surrounding areas and potentially flooding. Areas of gravel let water percolate into the soil, reducing flooding and providing damp soils for root systems and enhancing the soil ecosystem.

Native planting (plants originally from the UK) versus non-native planting has also been a hotly debated topic over recent years. Originally it was believed that native species were better for attracting wildlife. Whilst this is considered to be the case for the ability of trees to provide a wildlife habitat, recent studies have found little difference when looking at other plant species. For flowering plants, it was identified that having more flowers with nectar and pollen over a long season provided a more varied diet for pollinators than local flowers with a shorter lifespan. Therefore, a variety of native and non-native plant types would seem to be the most beneficial, incorporating shrubs, herbaceous perennials, climbers, bulbs, grasses and trees. In addition, a monoculture of one plant type can result in increased diseases and a prevalence of certain types of pests. Sustainability is determined by a balance, by allowing nature to take hold, but at the same time keeping an eye out for potential areas of dominance and conflict. If you notice one species taking over, it might be worth intervening a little to alter the balance so that nothing begins to get out of control.

Before doing anything to your garden, try to find out what wildlife is already in residence and might be disturbed if you start making radical changes. In a large garden, this may take 6–12 months as you wait to see which plants come up, what wildlife is attracted and if any nesting sites exist. Don't just consider the daytime visitors, check for nocturnal life including moths, hedgehogs, slugs and snails. If you are lucky enough to already have a pond or water feature, check for frog and toad spawn as well as any other aquatic life.

As it is difficult to observe your garden at all times of the day and night, you could use a camera trap to monitor your garden. Camera traps are generally inexpensive and once triggered by movement will photograph or record the action. People are often surprised about what

activity takes place in their garden without their knowledge.

When planning your planting, there are a number of points to consider. Firstly, your soil type (alkaline, neutral, or acid) and the underlying drainage (well drained, poorly drained) as these will impact on the type of plants you can grow. Secondly, the amount of space you have as you need to consider the final size and shape of the planting. Very large trees and shrubs can block out the light to other plants as well as your home and potentially your neighbours' property. Thirdly, the aspect of the garden in terms of the proportions of sun and shade in the garden will also impact on what will grow successfully. A shady, damp garden will be good for a woodland edge or wetland habitat, but not so useful for attracting bees and butterflies. Also note that some plants that thrive in the south-east of England may do less well in Scotland and the north of England.

You will also need to consider the wider food chain and ecosystem that you are trying to support.

Your garden is also your family's relaxation space, and any design should take account of each family member's activities. Consider what everyone wants and determine which of the requirements can be met. Are there any types of wildlife that family members do not want to encourage into the garden? Any garden, even a wildlife garden, will also require some maintenance. Who is going to do this and how much

time and effort will they want to spend on the task? Which tools will be required and where will they be stored?

Having considered all of these points, draw a plan of your garden by measuring the garden with a tape measure and then transferring the measurements using an appropriate scale onto paper or a tablet or desktop. For most gardens, a scale of around 1–2cm per metre tends to fit a standard sheet of A4 or A3 paper. Then you can start allocating space for specific purposes, such as meadow, paths, nectar border, compost bins, boundary hedges etc. In doing so, you need to consider the ecosystem you are trying to support in relation to the feeding, drinking and nesting/accommodation requirements of different species.

To assist in your planning, the remaining twelve chapters of this book will concentrate on four main areas:

1. Planting for wildlife in nectar-rich borders, wildflower meadows, hedgerows and in trees and shrubs
2. Building for wildlife with bird boxes, bug boxes, feeders and ponds
3. Green gardening approaches with fruit and vegetable production, rain gardens, green roofs, compost making and creating new plants through propagation
4. Attracting specific species of birds, bees, butterflies, other insects, aquatic life and nightlife.

CHAPTER 2

Creating a Nectar Border

'Where flowers bloom, so does hope'
LADY BIRD JOHNSON

Nectar borders offer sustenance to a wide range of pollinators such as birds, bees, butterflies, beetles, bats and other small mammals. These pollinators are important as they facilitate reproduction in 90 per cent of the world's flowering plants and trees. Nectar borders are rich in flowers, providing an attractive addition to the garden as well as providing breeding grounds for many varieties of insect species. There is nothing quite like exploring a floral border with a variety of shapes and colours and hearing the buzz of the busy bees. Typically, borders follow a fence, wall or hedge, but they don't need to be large, and even a balcony with nectar-rich plants in pots can attract and sustain many pollinators.

The Beneficiaries

Bee, butterfly, moth, ladybird, lacewing, spider, beetle, hoverfly, bat, song thrush, goldfinch, chaffinch, blue tit, great tit, hedgehog.

Establishing a Nectar Border

1. Selecting a Location

Survey your site and find a suitable location to have your border. Ideally, you want to find a location within your garden that is sunny and sheltered. It is therefore important to start by considering the direction your garden faces as this will

determine how much sun and shade your plants will receive. Is it south, east, west, or north facing? This will determine the best location for the border and which plants will flourish there.

South-facing gardens receive the most sun which may be beneficial for the majority of wildlife, but there may need to be some shady spots to provide some refuge for wildlife and the hard-working gardener. Depending on the size of the plot, this may mean putting some taller shrubs and trees in a border at the bottom of the garden whilst putting your nectar border in the sunnier middle of the garden or nearer the house.

East-facing gardens may be in full sun in the morning but in the shade by mid-afternoon. Therefore, any border close to the house may not be suitable as a nectar border as insects will move to other locations and even your neighbours' gardens when it gets shady.

West-facing gardens get the sun in the afternoon but are in the shade in the morning. Plant your nectar border away from the house to avoid the colder morning shade. If you have a wildlife pond, it may be important to ensure that it is far away from the house to allow newts, frogs and hoverflies to warm up in any morning sunshine before they get active.

North-facing gardens will get most sunshine the further you get from the house. So, nectar borders should be nearer the end of the garden to enable bees and other insects to receive the heat of the sun.

Do not worry if your garden is not very sunny as you can adapt the design with plants that are shade-loving and able to cope with these reduced light levels. It is also possibly an idea to position a garden seat or bench close to the border, as this will allow you to enjoy the sight of pollinators visiting the flowers. Nectar borders are also good at visually softening hard garden boundaries created by fences and walls.

Soil with good drainage is also important for a nectar border, as many of the nectar-rich plants thrive better in well-drained soil. If drainage is very poor and the soil is stony or

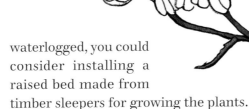

waterlogged, you could consider installing a raised bed made from timber sleepers for growing the plants.

Before you plant, especially if planting directly into the soil, remove any stones and weeds and consider adding an organic mulch to the soil. Organic mulches add some additional nutrients into the soil and are made from dead plant material such as compost, leaves, bark or grass clippings. They can also help to suppress weeds and retain moisture.

2. Selecting the Plants

The optimum time to plant a nectar border in the UK is in spring or autumn as planting at this time of year will reduce the need to water until they become established. Most commonly, perennials and biennials are grown in nectar borders. Perennials grow and flower for a number of years whereas biennials complete their life cycle over two years with foliage being created in the first year and flowers appearing in the second year before setting seed and dying off. Suitable plants could include:

Achillea ptarmica (sneezewort)
　　Clusters of pompom-shaped white flowers; height 0.5–1m; flowers June–August; prefers partial shade in a moist but well-drained soil

Achillea ptarmica (sneezewort)

Agastache foeniculum (anise hyssop)
: Short spikes of small violet-blue flowers; height 0.5–1m; flowers July–September; prefers full sun in well-drained soil

Aquilegia vulgaris (granny's bonnet)
: Usually blue 'nodding bonnets', but purple, pink and white colour variants are available; height 0.5–1m; flowers April–May; prefers sun or partial shade on moist but well-drained soil

Digitalis purpurea (foxglove)
: Spikes of pendant, tubular, pink/purple flowers; height 1.5–2.5m; flowers in early summer; prefers partial shade but will grow in full sun on almost any soil

Echinacea purpurea (cone flower)
: Pink flower heads with light purple rays and brown central disk; height 1–1.5m; flowers in late summer; prefers full sun but can tolerate some shade on well-drained humus-rich soil

Echium vulgare (viper's bugloss/adderwort)
: Spikes of blue funnel-shaped flowers; height 0.5–1m; flowers all summer; prefers full sun in moderately fertile well-drained soil

Geranium 'Rozanne'

Geranium 'Rozanne'
Saucer-shaped violet-blue flowers with a white centre; height 0.5–1m; flowers all summer; prefers full sun or partial shade on well-drained soil

Lavandula angustifolia (English lavender)
Spikes of small tubular blue/purple flowers with evergreen foliage; height 0.5–1m; flowers June–July; prefers full sun on well-drained soil

Nepeta 'Six Hills Giant' (catmint)
Aromatic leaves and spikes of tubular blue/purple flowers; height 0.5–1m; flowers in early summer; prefers full sun or partial shade in well-drained soil

Papaver rhoeas (poppy)
Bowl-shaped flowers on wiry stems. Various varieties with pink, white, red or peach flowers; height 0.5–1m; flowers all summer; prefers full sun on well-drained soil

Phacelia tanacetifolia (fiddleneck)
Fern-like leaves and densely set soft blue flowers; height 0.5–1m; flowers summer–autumn; prefers full sun on well-drained soil

Pulicaria dysenterica (common fleabane)
Clusters of yellow, daisy-like flower heads on long stems; height 0.5–1m; flowers July–September; prefers full sun or partial shade on heavy poorly drained soil

Papaver rhoeas (poppy)

Pulmonaria officinalis (lungwort)

Spotted greenish-white broad leaves with clusters of blue/ pink flowers; height 0.1–0.5m; flowers in early spring; prefers full or partial shade on humus-rich, moist soil

Scabiosa atropurpurea (pincushion flower)

Pincushion-like flower heads on wiry stems. Various varieties with blue, pink, red, black or purple flowers; height 40–70cm; flowers June–August; prefers full sun on well-drained soil

Silene dioica (red campion/adder's flower)

Deeply notched, pink petals on long stems; height 0.5–1m; flowers all summer; prefers partial shade on well-drained soil

Verbena bonariensis (purple top/Argentinian vervain)

Tall erect architectural plant with small purple flowers; height 1.5–2.5m; flowers in summer; prefers full sun in well-drained soil

Pulmonaria officinalis
(lungwort)

If you have enough space, you could also include a nectar-rich shrub such as a Buddleja, which is particularly attractive to butterflies. It is best to choose a range of plants where there is nectar available throughout the year if possible. A mixture

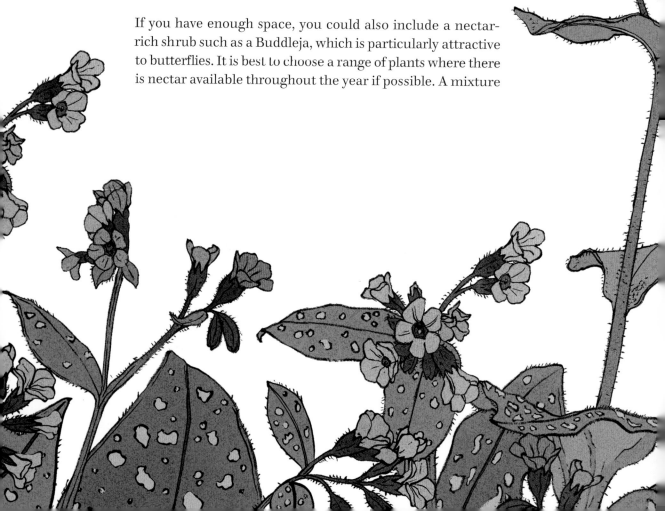

of native and non-native plants can be the best way of extending the flowering season of your border. Stage the plants by putting the tallest at the back working out towards the shortest at the front of the border. If, however, the bed is accessible from all sides, position the tallest plants in the middle and the smallest plants at the front of the border. Try to fill the entire area with plants as a smaller area of bare soil will result in less weeding in the future.

Colour combinations are extremely important in terms of garden design and the atmosphere you want to create in the garden. When designing gardens for wildlife and in particular for pollinators, their ability to locate and find appropriate flowers is important. It has been found that some insects see ultraviolet light better than other colours, so colours like blue, purple and pink are important to plant. Other insects can also pick up yellow and white flowers. Night-time pollinators often seek out white flowers. For this reason, it is important to have a range of different coloured flowers which can be planted in colourful drifts leading from one colour palette to another.

Scent is also important as it guides pollinators towards flowers, especially for insects like moths that visit flowers at night. Many flowers have evolved to flower at night when these pollinators are most active. It is also an added bonus to select plants that bring a sweet scent to your garden. These could include:

Nicotiana sylvestris (flowering tobacco)
Dark green leaves with dangling clusters of white flowers; height 1–1.5m; flowers in summer; prefers full sun or partial shade on well-drained moist soil
Magnolia grandiflora (magnolia)
Fragrant, cup-shaped, large cream flowers; height 12–15m; flowers in late summer/autumn; prefers full sun or partial shade on well-drained moist soil
Jasminum officinale (jasmine)
Scented star-shaped white flowers; height 4–8m; flowers in late summer/autumn; prefers full sun or partial shade on well-drained moist soil

Lilium regale (regal lily)
: Vigorous bulbous plant with narrow glossy green leaves and fragrant, trumpet-shaped white flowers, yellow in the centre and flushed with purple on the outside; height 1–1.5m; flowers in summer; prefers full sun on well-drained moist soil

Matthiola longipetala (night-scented stock)
: Small, grey-green leaves and white, purple, or pink flowers; height 0.1–0.5m; flowers in summer; prefers full sun on well-drained moist soil

Flower shape is also important, as not all plants provide a good source of nectar and pollen. So how do you track down the plants that do? It is best to look for simple structured plants that have single flowers. If a flower is very blousy and double-headed with multiple layers of petals, insects can find it very difficult to access the pollen. The stamens and petals are so modified that these plants cannot reproduce without human interference. Many of these plants have been bred to be showy to humans, rather than to assist our pollinators. For example, bees need flowers that have landing pad areas on the flowers with a single set of petals. It will help if the centre of the flower is highly visible to the pollinating insects. Many flowers, like foxgloves, also have nectar trails that guide the bee into the flower where the nectar is located. Many garden centres in the UK use the RHS Plants for Pollinators symbol on plants that are particularly suitable for nectar borders.

3. Ongoing Maintenance

Once the border has become established, you will need to check regularly for weeds. This might not be too much of a task as the plants grow and the amount of bare earth reduces. In terms of managing the plants, leave old growth over the winter as this provides a home for invertebrates and poten-

tially some seeds for birds. In early spring, you should cut them back as this prepares the plants for the new growing season. As the border matures after about 3–5 years, you may need to split some of the herbaceous perennials (plants whose growth dies down annually but whose roots or other underground parts survive) to prevent them becoming congested and woody in the centre. This can be done by digging up the plant and splitting the root with a spade, two forks back-to-back, or secateurs. The individual parts can then be replanted in different parts of the border or shared with friends and neighbours.

One of the best-known reasons for encouraging wildlife into your nectar border is that you will find the need for human intervention to control so-called pests throughout the rest of the garden is remarkably reduced. Aphids that may be attacking our roses in one part of the garden are likely to be predated upon by the ladybirds, hoverflies and birds that we have encouraged through planting the nectar border. A natural balance is created, and this helps us reduce the need for chemicals. This is not only important for the planet, but is also important as garden chemicals are experiencing increased restrictions and legislation. Also, it is worth noting that pesticides kill the good insects as well as the pests; slug pellets kill hedgehogs; and fungicides and weedkillers affect

earthworms. If additional steps are required, it is possible to use companion planting or biological controls. Companion planting is all about creating plant communities which have mutual benefits to each other. Nectar borders act as companion planting for the whole garden, but in specific areas, you can include plants such as herbs or marigolds, as their strongly scented leaves can help repel insects. French marigolds (*Tagetes patula*) are particularly good at keeping pests away from your tomato plants and nasturtiums (*Tropaeolum majus*) are good at protecting apples, brassicas and cucumbers.

Biological controls involve the use of natural enemies such as predators or pathogenic nematodes to control pests. Predatory and parasitoid

Tropaeolum majus (nasturtium) are good for protecting apples, brassicas and cucumbers from insect pests

biological controls rarely give instant reductions in prey populations as they need time to multiply. It is therefore important to introduce them before you have a heavy infestation of pests. However, you do need some of the pests to be present as the predators won't breed until they have pests to prey on. Generally, biological controls are supplied by mail order and can be used to deal with major infestations of pests such as aphids, carrot fly, leather jackets, slugs, cabbage root fly, gooseberry sawfly and vine weevil.

If you find that certain plants are diseased, the best form of control is to remove the infected parts of plants as soon as they are seen. The infected material should be burnt immediately or removed from the garden. Do not put it in your compost bin as the heat in the bin may not be sufficient to kill the spores of the fungi causing the disease, and so you could end up spreading the disease around the garden.

The vine weevil, an insect that feeds on a wide range of plants and fruits

CHAPTER 3
Planting a Wildflower Meadow

'How does the Meadow flower its bloom unfold?
Because the lovely little flower is free down to its root,
and in that freedom bold'
WILLIAM WORDSWORTH

Rethinking Your Lawn

Changing the way we maintain and manage our traditional lawns will help encourage more wildlife into our gardens. In the past we have mown our lawns regularly throughout the growing season. This typically would start in the spring or late winter and mowing continues right through until the first frosts in the autumn. The only time we allow our lawns to rest is during the winter months. Sustainable gardening means that we don't necessarily need to have the perfect green lawn, which has been a national obsession for centuries in our gardens. These manicured lawns have resulted in a few grasses dominating, with low-growing flowers, sometimes referred to as weeds, being removed. They provide no resources for bees, flies, moths, butterflies, wasps and beetles, which rely on a rich diet of pollen and nectar, and there is little structure for insects and other invertebrates to shelter. They also require a lot of maintenance as we feed them and weed them with chemicals and then we mow them often on a weekly basis. Nowadays for many people,

31

petrol and electric mowers and strimmers are used adding to our carbon footprint and damaging the planet.

A slight rethink on how we design and maintain our lawns could have a big impact for our wildlife and in particular, our wildflower species. They need more help than ever due to the destruction of their habitat in the countryside. Experts say 97 per cent of the UK's meadows have been eradicated since the 1930s. The lawn in people's gardens could once again play its part in a functioning ecosystem with insects, small mammals and birds feeding on it, building their homes in it, or using it as a source of nesting materials. Developing a wildlife habitat in your lawn can be as easy as raising the height at which you cut the grass; cutting less frequently or leaving a patch of grass where you do not cut. Some people leave much of their lawn uncut and simply mow attractive paths through the unmown grass. Alternatively, you can sow a species-rich wildflower meadow mix native to your local region. Wildflower meadows can provide a valuable resource

Leucanthemum vulgare (ox-eye daisy), left, and *Plantago lanceolata* (ribwort plantain), right

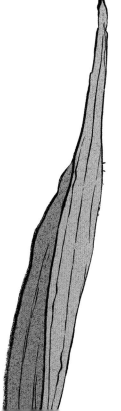

for pollinators as well as a landscape that is both colourful and aesthetically pleasing. You do not need to change all your lawn into a wildflower meadow, it is just as worthwhile to change a small section or patch whilst keeping the remainder of the lawn for ball games and children playing.

The term 'wildflower meadows' is often used to refer to areas of perennial or annual meadow plants. Annual meadow plants consisting of cornfield annuals tend to be planted in borders similar to the nectar border in the previous chapter. Perennial meadows which will come up every year are meadows where grasses and flowers combine and compete and tend to thrive best in poorer-quality soils.

The Beneficiaries

Bee, butterfly, ladybird, moth, hoverfly, beetle, blackbird, lizard, shrew, slow worm.

Establishing a Wildflower Meadow

Sadly, wildflower meadows have often had a bad reputation for being difficult to achieve and establish. Soil condition is the main determinant of a successful wildflower meadow. They work best on soils that are poor in nutrients. If there is too much fertility in the soil, they may thrive for a short time but will then be taken over by weeds and coarse grasses. For this reason, the soil in your standard lawn will be too nutrient rich, particularly if you have been feeding your lawn, and also as grass can be high in nitrogen when it breaks down.

The following steps should therefore be followed if you want to develop a perennial wildflower meadow:

1. Preparing the Soil

Start by stripping the turf and topsoil off the area that you want to turn into meadow. It is probably best to do all of this when the ground is dry. Digging down to around 15cm will take you to the subsoil, and this should be less fertile than the topsoil immediately under the lawn. You can either remove topsoil to a border or you can dig up some subsoil and mix it with this topsoil before replacing it and keeping the levels of your garden the same. Remove any stones and weeds that are in the soil.

2. Planting the Seed

It is best to sow wildflowers in the spring or the autumn. The first plant that should be included in your meadow is yellow rattle (*Rhinanthus minor*), which is a parasitic plant that helps weaken the grass. This in turn will allow other wildflowers to establish in the ideal conditions for them to thrive and grow. The prepared seed mixes that are available tend to be a combination of around 70–80 per cent wild grass species and 20–30 per cent wild-flowers. They typically include plants such as:

Achillea millefolium (yarrow)
    Feathery foliage and flat headed pink flowers; height 0.1–0.5m; flowers early summer–early autumn; prefers full sun on well-drained moist soil
Agrimonia eupatoria (agrimony)
    Erect plant with yellow flower spikes; height 0.1–0.5m; flowers June–August; prefers full sun or partial shade on well-drained moist soil

Rhinanthus minor (yellow rattle)

Primula florindae
(Tibetan cowslip)

Centaurea nigra (common knapweed)
Upright plant with thistle-like purple flower heads; height 0.5–0.7m; flowers June–September; prefers full sun or partial shade on well-drained moist soil

Origanum vulgare (English marjoram)
A bushy plant with small aromatic leaves and clusters of small pink flowers; height 0.5–1m; flowers in summer and early autumn; prefers full sun or partial shade on well-drained soil

Plantago lanceolata (ribwort plantain)
Low-growing plant with leafless spikes or brown flowers with white antlers and rosettes of ribbed green leaves; height 0.1–0.5m; flowers in summer; prefers full sun on well-drained moist soil

Primula florindae (Tibetan cowslip)
Erect stems with broad leaves carrying bunches of nodding yellow flowers; height 1–1.2m; flowers in summer; prefers full sun or partial shade on well-drained moist soil

Rhinanthus minor (yellow rattle)
Leafy spikes of tubular yellow flowers with inflated calyx; height 0.1–0.5m; flowers in summer; prefers full sun on well-drained moist soil

Silene vulgaris (bladder campion)
Upright plant with oval leaves and white flowers each with an inflated calyx; height 0.3–0.6m; flowers in early summer; prefers full sun or partial shade on well-drained moist soil

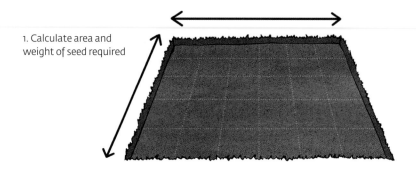

1. Calculate area and weight of seed required

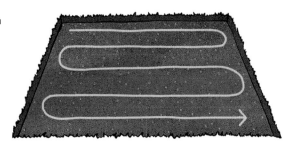

2. Sow half of seed in one direction

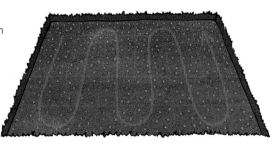

3. Sow rest of seed in opposite direction then rake / flatten and net

4. Established meadow

Seed suppliers should be able to suggest the best seed mixes for the climatic conditions in your area. You can also include biennials such as teasel (*Dipsacus fullonum*), wild carrot (*Daucus carota*) and ox-eye daisies (*Leucanthemum vulgare*), although these will need to be resown every two years.

The seed should be sown at the rate suggested by the seed supplier, but this is usually around 4–5 grams per square metre. You can mix the seed with sand to make it easier to sow by hand, or if it is a large area you may want to use a seed broadcaster. It is often best to sow the seeds in one direction across the area and then sow across the area again in a direction that is 90 degrees to the first sowing. After spreading the seed, you should rake the soil or gently flatten the soil with your feet in order to press the seeds into full contact with the soil. Then keep animals and people off the site for around 4–6 weeks. You may also need to put a net over the site to stop pigeons feeding on your seed.

3. Maintaining the Meadow

At first, the meadow may look like an untidy patch of grasses and weeds, but it will soon establish itself and the flowers and wildlife will start to dominate. Cut back the meadow once a year in the late summer/autumn. Do this once most of the wildflowers have set seed. Leave the cuttings for a few days to give them time to dry and drop their seeds. After that, it is best to rake off the clippings to reduce nutrients breaking down and going back into the soil. Scratching the surface of the meadow with a rake in the autumn will also help to remove thatch and will expose bare patches so that the wildflower seed has the ability to establish in these gaps. The cuttings from the meadow can either be left in quiet corners of the garden as a potential habitat for wildlife or can be added to the compost bin. By limiting the cutting to once per year, you will be supporting a greater variety of plant and animal species within the meadow area. In later years, you may use plug plants to add additional species to an existing meadow.

A Flowering Lawn

If you don't want to go as far as creating a wildflower meadow, you could simply introduce wildflowers into an existing lawn. A trial at the Royal Botanic Garden Edinburgh (RBGE) looked at how 'flowering' lawns can be created to provide habitats for wildlife and become more colourful and attractive at the same time. The research project, part of the Edinburgh Living Landscape (ELL) strategy to improve the city for nature, has resulted in the creation of two success-ful trial plots at RBGE providing a low sward that can be used like a traditional lawn but with many more flowers. The cutting height is around 5cm and plants that will flower below this height are included in the lawn.

The best times to create such a lawn are early spring and autumn. The plants are usually bought as plug plants. You need to first cut the lawn on the mower's lowest setting and then rake over the lawn. This removes any thatch and moss and will open up bare areas for the plug plants. It is probably best to have a mixture of plants and you should aim to arrange them on the lawn before planting. A trowel can then be used to dig a small hole for each plug plant. Possible plants include:

Lotus corniculatus (bird's foot trefoil)
> Low-level plant with yellow-coloured flowers; height 0.1–0.2m; flowers late spring–early autumn; prefers full sun on well-drained soil

Primula florindae (Tibetan cowslip)
> Erect stems with broad leaves carrying bunches of nodding yellow flowers; height 1–1.2m; flowers July–August; prefers full sun or partial shade on well-drained moist soil

Primula vulgaris (wild primrose)
> Plant with light green leaves and fragrant, long-stalked yellow flowers; height 0.1–0.3m; flowers March–May; prefers full sun or partial shade on well-drained moist soil

Ranunculus acris (meadow buttercup)

Upright plant with long-stalks and bright glossy yellow, bowl-shaped flowers; height 0.5–0.8m; flowers June–July; prefers full sun or partial shade on well-drained moist soil

Trifolium pratense (red clover)

Small creeping plant with clusters of pinkish-red flowers; height 0.1–0.3m; flowers May–September; prefers full sun on well-drained moist soil

Planting naturalised bulbs like camassias and daffodils in drifts through the lawn can also provide attractive spring interest.

In terms of maintenance, leave the area for around a month before mowing. You can then mow around them for another month to let them get established and ultimately you can mow over the top of them on a regular basis using a high setting on your mower. Each year, aim to keep the grass surrounding the plants under control with the mower in the spring which then allows the flowers to grow and flower for six to eight weeks in the summer.

Trifolium pratense
(red clover)

CHAPTER 4

Creating a Native Hedgerow or Wildlife Fence

'A hedge between keeps friendship green'
PROVERB

In basic terms, a hedge is a line of plants that are pruned into a particular formal shape to provide a boundary in your garden. As the above proverb suggests, a hedge can keep relationships with your neighbours green, but it can also be green for the environment. Hedges are known for being key in helping to attract wildlife into your garden. They can be low maintenance and may only require a once-a-year clip to keep looking neat and tidy.

Malus sylvestris (crab apple)

In practical terms, a boundary to your garden can be any size and made from any material. A mixture of materials will benefit your local wildlife to its best potential. An urban street of houses, each with a hedge or fence with climbers or even a boundary created by a grove of small trees will provide a wildlife corridor for birds, insects and other animals to move between gardens. Hedges, trees and climbers can provide nesting sites and a food source. Even a dry stone wall can provide a home for insects, birds and small mammals.

Almost any boundary in your garden can be enhanced to

provide food, shelter and habitat for wildlife. Some examples are adding climbers to fences for birds to nest in and feed on, and these climbers might flower, providing pollinators with nectar and pollen. During the bird-breeding season, certain species of birds like yellowhammers rely solely on hedgerows to build their nests and raise their young. You can also easily add insect boxes to a stone wall using twigs, straw and pine cones which will provide a habitat and refuge for them. It has even been found that bats use hedgerows and walls as land-marks to navigate whilst feeding on insects during dusk.

Some of the best hedges are ones that have thorns, as this will prevent predators accessing nests. Those that produce flowers for pollinators should also be encouraged. These flowers will then turn into food in the form of fruit or seeds for wildlife to eat over the winter months.

Remember, hedges and wild fences can be used within a garden to screen off bins, sheds and other areas in addition to acting as a boundary with your neighbours.

Birds like the yellowhammer rely on hedgerows for nesting

The Beneficiaries

Blackbird, robin, wren, great tit, blue tit, dunnock, butterfly, moth, bee, hedgehog, shrew, wood mouse.

Planting the Hedge

It is best to plant your hedge in the autumn. Prepare your ground so that it is root free and the soil is evenly broken up so that you can make planting holes. As a rough guideline, you want to space the plants in a hedge at about 30cm apart in a single continuous row. Planting is just like planting a tree or shrub, where you will dig a large hole that is big enough for the plant's roots and ensure that the soil that you plant into is not compacted in any way. Backfill the planting hole with the surrounding soil and gently firm the soil with the heel of your garden boot. If it is a mixed hedge of different species, you might want to group each species in a block before moving on to the next plant species. In time, the plants will fill out the space and produce a dense hedge and attractive boundary in your garden. It is best to water any newly planted hedge and keep it watered during its first year, particularly during hot and dry periods of weather.

EXAMPLES OF WILDLIFE HEDGE SPECIES

Taxus baccata (yew)
  Year-round evergreen coverage for nesting birds and fruit for birds on female plants
Crataegus monogyna (hawthorn)
  Produces large amounts of tiny flowers in spring for pollinators and then the fruits can feed birds and mammals in the winter
Malus sylvestris (crab apple)
  Provides blossom and fruit for birds
Prunus spinosa (blackthorn)
  This hedge bears thorns that will protect wildlife and has attractive blossom in spring helping pollinators. The fruit (sloes) can feed birds in the autumn

Rosea canina
(dog-rose)

Ilex (holly)

    Provides year-round evergreen cover for nesting birds to hide from predators and the fruit on the female plant species can feed birds in the winter

Fagus (beech)

    Leaves turn a lovely copper colour in autumn and stay on all winter, which acts as a safe place for nesting birds needing cover and protection

Ribes sanguineum (flowering currant)

    Provides spring flowers for pollinators and fruits later in the season for mammals and birds

Rosea canina (dog-rose)

    Dog roses are best with open flowers that allow pollinators to feed on the nectar and pollen. The thorny species will provide safe shelter for nesting birds and the hips can provide food for birds

Corylus (hazel)

    Its leaves are eaten by caterpillars and moths. The branches can also be laid horizontally, providing good shelter for small mammals and birds

Berberis darwinii (barberry)
    Has spiky branches that provide safe nesting sites and the flowers can provide a source of nectar for pollinators

LOOKING AFTER YOUR HEDGE

Once your hedge is planted in the autumn, you can sit back and wait for it to start growing in the spring. On many deciduous species, new leaves will emerge around April. Make sure the hedge line is kept weed free as weeds can act as competition for nutrients while the hedge is trying to get established. By year two, the hedge will be growing strongly and be ready for some cutting back in the autumn/early winter months. This cutting will keep the hedge in shape and ensure it thickens up well. If you want to minimise wildlife disturbance you may consider cutting the hedgerow every two years, particularly if you are in a less formal garden setting.

Wild Fences

The many varieties of clematis are perfect for a wild fence

If a hedge isn't appropriate as you want immediate privacy from your neighbours or you want to keep their dog out of your garden, then a wildlife fence may be the answer. A wild fence is simply a fence with climbers growing up it. To provide support for the climbing plants, simply attach a wooden trellis or wires to an existing fence. Then choose climbing plants such as:

Clematis

Many varieties in colours including pinks, purples and whites; height 4–8m; flowers dependant on the variety in spring, summer or autumn; prefers full sun or partial shade on well-drained moist soil

Lonicera sempervirens (trumpet honeysuckle)
Blue-green leaves with orange-red flowers followed by red berries; height 2–4m; flowers spring–autumn; prefers full sun or partial shade on well-drained moist soil

Passiflora caerulea (passion flower)
Lobed leaves and flowers with intricate pattern of blue, purple and white; height 8–12m; flowers June–September; prefers full sun or partial shade on well-drained moist soil

Jasminum officinale (jasmine)
Scented star-shaped white flowers; height 4–8m; flowers late summer/autumn; prefers full sun or partial shade on well-drained moist soil

Rosa (climbing rose)
Many varieties of climbing rose in a variety of colours of solitary or clustered flowers; height 1.5–3m; flowers in summer; prefers full sun or partial shade on well-drained moist soil

Pyracantha (firethorn)
Evergreen with spiny branches, small leaves and small white flowers followed by red, orange or yellow berries; height 2–4m; flowers in June; prefers full sun or partial shade on well-drained moist soil

These should be planted close to the fence in spring or autumn and attached to the trellis or wires with garden twine. As the plants grow, tie them in further up the fence. Water the plants well in their first season and add mulch to the base of the climbers each year. Small birds, such as wrens, and insects will often find themselves a home within the branches of the climber or between the climber and the fence.

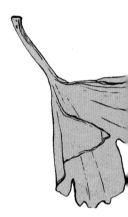

CHAPTER 5

Planting Trees and Shrubs for Wildlife

'The best time to plant a tree is twenty years ago.
The second best time is now'
CHINESE PROVERB

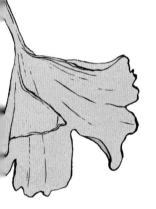

If your garden is big enough, trees and shrubs can offer many benefits for wildlife. Mature trees provide safe homes and perches for wildlife above many predators. Insects live on the branches or inside the wood, providing food for birds. Moss, twigs, and autumn leaves can provide nesting materials for many birds and mammals. Even small trees and shrubs can shelter wildlife from rain and wind as well as providing fruits, nuts, and flowers for sustenance.

In terms of global warming, trees and shrubs are also very important in capturing carbon dioxide and producing the oxygen we breathe. They can also reduce flooding by absorbing large amounts of water from the surrounding soil, and in the autumn their falling leaves provide nutrients for the soil.

Native tree species are probably best at supporting wildlife, as they support more insects and grubs that birds and mammals feed on. Broadleaf trees tend to offer more for wildlife than conifers because they produce flowers and potentially fruit as well as leaf litter in the autumn. Conifers tend to be faster growing, but do not produce true flowers for pollinators, however, being evergreen, they do offer protection to wildlife in the winter.

Shrubs can also provide valuable nesting sites for birds and insects as well as provide attractive foliage, stunning flowers and remarkable stem colours. In choosing shrubs for your garden, you should be aiming for a diverse mix which can support wildlife as well as being pleasing to the eye.

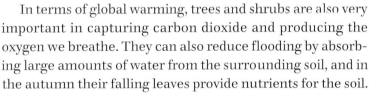

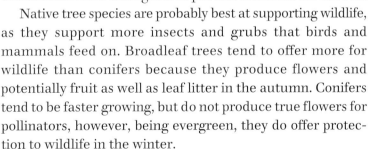

The Beneficiaries

All species of bird, bat, hedgehog, butterfly, moth, spider, bee, squirrel, wood mouse.

Selecting a Tree

When selecting a tree, look around your neighbourhood to see which trees seem to thrive in the soil and climatic conditions in your area. Buy a UK-sourced tree as this is less likely to bring in pests and diseases from other countries. Generally, it is best to choose saplings that are around one to two years old, as planting at that stage is likely to result in a mature tree that is stronger and healthier. However, it is important to consider the likely ultimate size of the mature tree. What may start as a small sapling could result in a 20-metre tree that dominates your whole garden blocking out all sunshine and upsetting your neighbours.

How to Plant a Tree

1. Purchase small specimens, as they are easier to establish than large expensive trees. A small tree will grow quickly and will normally become a fine specimen in around five years. Uprooting large trees makes them more prone to shock, and will require a lot of irrigation and staking to get them to establish and put down new roots.

2. Planting a tree while it is in full leaf or flower can put it under stress. Always plant trees in the autumn or winter as it gives them the opportunity to settle into their new surroundings by allowing them to anchor in the soil and find nutrients, and then they can slowly burst into life in the spring months. Planting at this time of year also means there is more likelihood of regular rainfall to keep the tree hydrated until its roots become established.

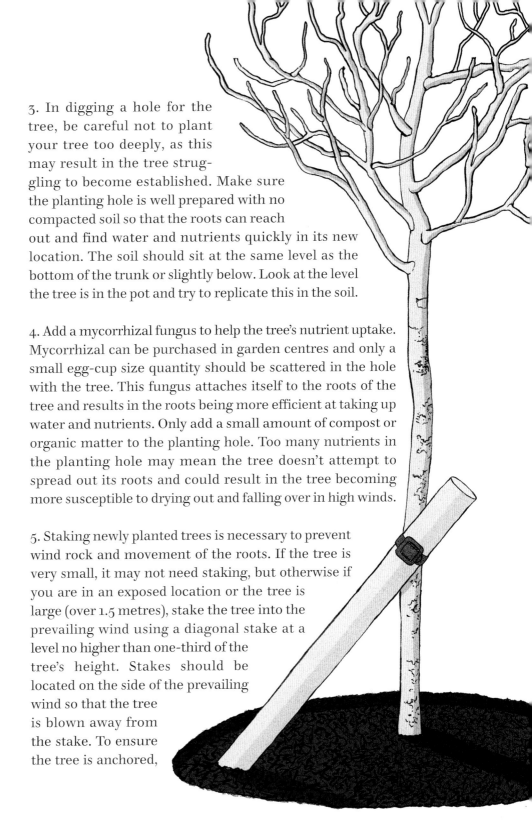

3. In digging a hole for the tree, be careful not to plant your tree too deeply, as this may result in the tree struggling to become established. Make sure the planting hole is well prepared with no compacted soil so that the roots can reach out and find water and nutrients quickly in its new location. The soil should sit at the same level as the bottom of the trunk or slightly below. Look at the level the tree is in the pot and try to replicate this in the soil.

4. Add a mycorrhizal fungus to help the tree's nutrient uptake. Mycorrhizal can be purchased in garden centres and only a small egg-cup size quantity should be scattered in the hole with the tree. This fungus attaches itself to the roots of the tree and results in the roots being more efficient at taking up water and nutrients. Only add a small amount of compost or organic matter to the planting hole. Too many nutrients in the planting hole may mean the tree doesn't attempt to spread out its roots and could result in the tree becoming more susceptible to drying out and falling over in high winds.

5. Staking newly planted trees is necessary to prevent wind rock and movement of the roots. If the tree is very small, it may not need staking, but otherwise if you are in an exposed location or the tree is large (over 1.5 metres), stake the tree into the prevailing wind using a diagonal stake at a level no higher than one-third of the tree's height. Stakes should be located on the side of the prevailing wind so that the tree is blown away from the stake. To ensure the tree is anchored,

stakes should penetrate the soil to at least 50–60cm. Tree ties are available to attach the tree to the stake and are made of durable, long-lasting plastic, with buckles for adjustment. These ties usually come with spacers to prevent the stem and stake from rubbing against each other. Make a figure of eight to hold the tree to the stake, with the spacer in between the tree and the stake, and secure the tie to the stake with a nail. The ties can be loosened as the tree expands in girth. Although the tree should be firmly anchored, the upper trunk and branches should still be allowed to move in the wind. This rocking movement in the wind enables the tree trunk to thicken and stand up to strong winds. Check the ties regularly for rubbing and adjust if necessary. As the tree grows, the ties will need to be loosened and adjusted. Once the tree becomes established after 3–5 years the tree stake can probably be removed, and it will be happy to grow away with no additional support. If your garden is regularly visited by deer or rabbits, it may be necessary to buy a tree guard/protector to stop the tree being eaten before it becomes established. The tree guard should be removed once the tree's trunk is strong with a diameter of around 4–5cm.

6. Pouring two large watering cans over the newly planted tree will help the tree roots make contact with the soil and start growing. During the first year, make sure you give the tree regular irrigation, particularly through the dry periods in the summer.

A Coppice Belt

In a larger garden it may be possible to introduce a coppice belt of trees. Coppicing is a traditional method for managing woodlands and involves regularly cutting down trees to a stump just above ground level. This severe form of pruning is usually undertaken every five to seven years during the winter, and promotes dense new growth whilst allowing light onto the woodland floor. The aim is to have a mix of native trees providing food and shelter for birds and small mammals.

1. Hazel tree prior to coppicing

2. Cut to around 7–10cm in winter

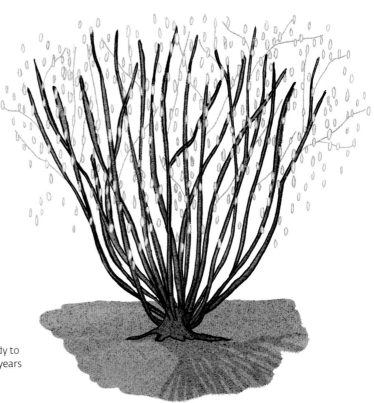

3. Shoots rapidly regrow creating more stems ready to be coppiced again in 5–7 years

Hyacinthoides-non-scripta (bluebell)

The selection of the mix should take account of different growth habits and vigour to produce a combination that reflects a natural woodland. For example, mixing birch or rowan trees with alder, hazel or holly. Diversity is important as different trees will be coppiced back at different times and will attract different wildlife. As the trees will be coppiced, the potential height of a tree is less important than a consideration of the overall spread of the plants relative to the space available. In general, the trees should be spaced around 2m apart, as this will give them room to grow and will also make it easier to coppice them when necessary.

The coppice belt requires little or no management in the first four to five years. Once the tallest trees have reached a preferred maximum height, around one fifth of the trees should be cut down to create a stump of around 7–10cm. The stumps will regenerate in the spring and develop new branches. Undertaking a similar task each year will ensure there is a balance of regenerating younger growth and more mature material. The coppiced branches can be used to create log piles or a dead hedge, which is a barrier constructed from cut branches, saplings, and foliage. This can be used to provide a boundary for the coppiced belt and, in addition, the leaf litter and twigs shed from the trees will offer habitats for insects, small mammals and birds.

A Woodland Glade

Many gardens have well-established trees on their boundaries. However, as a result, dense shade coupled with dry conditions can make gardening tricky in these areas. Creating a woodland glade can provide the answer to this problem. A woodland glade can be very attractive with flowering foxgloves, bluebells, wild garlic and primroses. These native plants have adapted to growing in dappled shade under a tree canopy and require little maintenance. They provide a shady, nectar-rich glade that offers a wonderful habitat for invertebrates to thrive as well as nectar-rich plants for pollinators. You can establish a glade with plug plants, bulbs in the green (bulbs with their leaves just beginning to die back) or from native woodland edge seed. Various bulbous plants, including *Galanthus nivalis* (snowdrops) and *Hyacinthoides non-scripta* (bluebells), are much easier to establish when planted in the green (after flowering) rather than as dry bulbs. Such plants are not always easy to get hold off, but you may find friends who have clumps to spare, and they are also obtainable from specialist nurseries. Do not be tempted to dig up these bulbs in the wild because it is against the law. Bluebells, in particular, will multiply quickly, and small clumps will soon spread to produce an attractive blue carpet of flowers in the spring. Clear any previous unwanted vegetation before planting. When it comes to the maintenance of a glade it is very straightforward – just cut it in late summer, allowing any seed to shake off into the ground then rake off the area and dress with compost. If any areas have failed or are bare you can add additional plug plants or seed mix each year.

Shrubs for Wildlife

By planting a variety of shrubs, you can provide year-round support for a vast array of wildlife to thrive in your garden. Some excellent examples are hawthorn, holly and cotoneaster. If you are looking to attract butterflies into your garden, plant shrubs that they will feed on during the summer months. Some native shrubs are needed for butterflies to feed on and lay their eggs to complete their life cycle. A popular shrub that is used to attract butterflies is buddleja, also known as the butterfly bush.

Shrubs come in many varieties of shape and size. They can be deciduous, evergreen and semi-evergreen, meaning it is possible to find ones to suit a wide range of sites. Selecting the right shrub for the right place and soil conditions is important if your shrub is to thrive once planted. The plant's label in the garden centre should indicate the growing conditions it requires in the garden. Generally, shrubs are reliable and easy to plant successfully, but some from native or warmer climates may suffer in cold winters and need the shelter of a wall or hedge. There are also ericaceous (lime-hating) shrubs, including rhododendrons and camellia, which tend to thrive better in a moist acid soil. In addition to buying an established shrub, it is also possible to grow a shrub from cuttings or seeds.

Once established, shrubs need only limited maintenance, feeding with compost and possibly mulching the soil with wood chips should maintain their growth. Removing dead flowers from the plants will also be beneficial. Once a year, it is likely to be necessary to prune the shrubs. In particular, deciduous shrubs that flower in late winter, spring and early summer need annual pruning to encourage strong, healthy shoots and improve flowering. The aim is to remove diseased, damaged, congested branches or shoots that are growing in unwanted directions. This can also result in more aesthetically pleasing shapes in your border. The timing to undertake the pruning will vary from one species of shrub to another.

SMALL TREES AND SHRUBS
(2–5 METRES IN HEIGHT)

Malus sylvestris
(crab apple)

Berberis vulgaris (barberry)
Deciduous, prickly shrub with orange-yellow flowers, followed by edible red fruits

Buddleja davidii (butterfly bush)
Upright shrub with arching branches and pink/purple flowers

Buxus sempervirens (box)
Slow-growing evergreen shrub with small glossy leaves and clusters of small, pale-yellow flowers, followed by pale-green to brown fruits

Cornus sanguinea (dogwood)
Deciduous with brightly coloured red stems in winter. Tiny white flowers with leaves turning orange-yellow in autumn

Cotoneaster simonsii (Himalayan cotoneaster)
Upright, semi-evergreen with small, glossy leaves and white flowers, followed by bright scarlet berries in autumn

Euonymus europaeus (spindle)
Dark green leaves developing bronze tints in autumn. Small nectar-rich green and white flowers, followed by pink fruit, splitting to reveal orange seeds in late autumn/ winter

Frangula alnus (alder buckthorn)
Deciduous with glossy leaves which turn yellow or red in autumn, small flowers in late spring and early summer, followed by red berries which ripen to black

Ilex aquifolium (holly)

    Evergreen with glossy, dark green, spiky leaves. Bright red berries in autumn/winter

Ligustrum vulgare (wild privet)

    Deciduous with dull green leaves and small, white flowers in summer, followed by small black berries

Malus sylvestris (crab apple)

    Deciduous with clusters of pink-tinged white flowers in late spring, followed by small yellow-green or red edible fruits

Prunus spinosa (blackthorn)
Deciduous thorny tree with dark green leaves and small white flowers in early spring followed by small black fruits

Prunus insititia (damson/bullace)
Deciduous tree with small, white flowers in early spring, followed by yellow, red, green or purple edible fruit

Rhamnus cathartica (purging buckthorn)
Deciduous small tree with glossy dark green leaves and small clusters of tiny yellowish flowers followed by red berries which ripen to black

Rosa canina (dog rose)
Deciduous with mid-green foliage and pale pink or white flowers in early summer, followed by red fruits

Rubus fruticosus (bramble/blackberry)
Deciduous with thorny long arching canes supporting white flowers and edible black berries

Sambucus nigra (elder)
Deciduous with golden-yellow leaves and creamy-white/ pink flowers followed by red, white or black edible berries

Sorbus aria (whitebeam)
Deciduous with dark green leaves, white-felted beneath and clusters of small white or pink flowers, followed by edible white, yellow, pink, red or brown berries

Taxus baccata (yew)
Evergreen with dense, linear leaves, insignificant flowers and, on female plants, red covering on the seeds

Ulex europaeus (common gorse)
Evergreen with spiny branches bearing small leaves and fragrant, yellow flowers followed by black seedpods

Viburnum lantana (wayfaring tree)
Deciduous with grey–green leaves and clusters of small tubular white flowers in late spring, followed by red fruits which ripen to black

Viburnum opulus 'Xanthocarpum' (guelder rose)
Deciduous with maple-like leaves turning yellow or pinkish in autumn. Creamy-white flowers are followed by translucent deep yellow berries

MEDIUM-SIZED TREES AND SHRUBS
(5–15 METRES IN HEIGHT)

Acer campestre (field maple)
    Deciduous with bushy leaves, turning yellow or red in the
    autumn. Small green flowers forming winged fruits
Corylus avellana 'Contorta' (corkscrew hazel)
    Deciduous with twisted branches bearing pendent yellow
    catkins
Crataegus monogyna (hawthorn)
    Deciduous with spiny branches and clusters of cream
    flowers, followed by red berries
Prunus padus 'Watereri' (bird cherry)
    Deciduous with green leaves turning yellow in autumn.
    Small, fragrant white flowers, followed by small black
    berries
Pyrus pyraster (wild pear)
    Deciduous with white blossom, followed by hard and
    inedible pears
Salix caprea (goat willow)
    Deciduous with broad leaves greyish beneath, and large
    grey catkins in spring
Sorbus aucuparia (rowan)
    Deciduous with clusters of small white or pink flowers,
    followed by white, pink, yellow, red, or brown berries

LARGE TREES
(OVER 15 METRES IN HEIGHT)

Aesculus hippocastanum (horse chestnut)
  Deciduous with large leaves, creamy-white flowers and large spiny fruit

Alnus glutinosa (alder)
  Deciduous with bright-green leaves, grey-purple buds and young catkins in winter

Betula pendula (silver birch)
  Deciduous, often with striking white, pink, or peeling brown bark. Catkins open before or with the leaves in spring

Carpinus betulus (hornbeam)
  Deciduous with attractive foliage and hop-like fruit clusters in late summer and autumn

Castanea sativa (sweet chestnut)
  Deciduous with grooved bark, long, glossy, toothed leaves and yellow catkins, followed by spiny fruits

Fagus sylvatica (beech)
  Deciduous with smooth grey bark, dark green leaves and spiny fruits

Fraxinus excelsior (ash)
  Deciduous with pale brown bark, dark green leaves and winged fruits in late summer and autumn

Larix decidua (European larch)
  Deciduous conifer with needle-like leaves and small erect cones. Leaves turn yellow in autumn

Pinus sylvestris (Scots pine)
  Evergreen with attractive bark, needle-like leaves and cones which remain on the tree for years

Populus nigra (black poplar)
  Deciduous narrow columnar tree with catkins opening before the leaves open in early spring. Male catkins are the more ornamental; female ones can be a nuisance from the cottony, wind-blown seeds

Populus tremula (aspen)
  Deciduous with catkins opening before the rounded leaves. Male catkins are the more ornamental; female ones can be a nuisance from the cottony, wind-blown seeds. Leaves are bronze when young and turn yellow in autumn

Quercus robur (English oak)
  Deciduous with a broad crown consisting of green leaves turning reddish-brown in autumn. Produces acorns

Salix alba (white willow)
  Deciduous with dark grey bark, dull green leaves that can appear silvery-white from a distance. Catkins appear with the leaves in spring

Tilia platyphyllos (large-leaved lime)
  Deciduous with heart-shaped leaves and clusters of fragrant yellow–green flowers, followed by winged fruits

Ulmus glabra (wych elm)
  Deciduous with red/purple flowers appearing before the leaves in early spring. Toothed leaves and small winged fruits

Ulmus procera (English elm)
  Deciduous with dark pink to red flowers that hang in tassels, appearing in early spring. Toothed leaves and small winged fruits

CHAPTER 6

Bug Houses,
Bird Boxes and Feeders

'Wherever I fly from my own dear nest,
I always come back, for home is the best'
MAUD LINDSAY

The planting that we have covered in the previous five chapters will bring life into your garden, but you can do more to encourage the wildlife to visit and potentially take up residence. You can provide homes and feeding stations in your garden for all sorts of insects, birds and mammals. This may be as simple as creating a log pile or investing time or money in constructing or buying bird boxes and feeders. Locating bird boxes for blue tits or homes for ladybirds and lacewings close to rose beds, for example, will help to reduce the number of pests as the residents in these dwellings will feed on aphids and greenfly.

The Beneficiaries

All types of insects, birds, mammals and invertebrates.

Building a Log Pile to Encourage Biodiversity

Any heap of garden material can provide a home or area of safety for wildlife. A pile of cut branches, hay or cut vegetation in a corner of the garden can provide a hibernation site for hedgehogs and small mammals such as shrews. Topping up the pile each autumn maintains the habitat and is better for the environment than having a bonfire. A pile of logs will provide the ideal habitat for small mammals, amphibians and the large number of insects that feed on wood or predate the

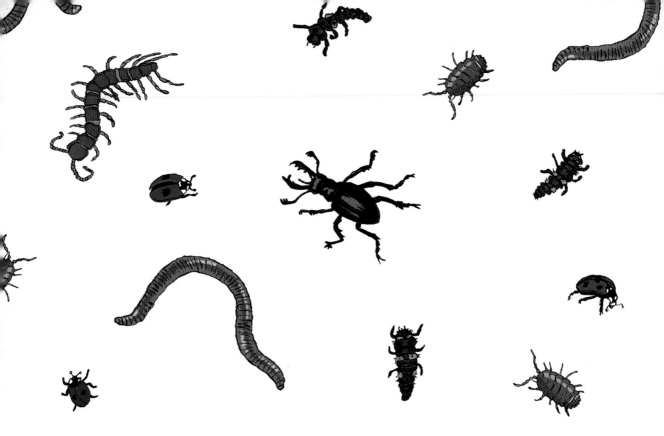

bugs that do. If you choose to stack your logs in a manner that resembles a tepee, the log pile can become suitable for larger animals such as hibernating hedgehogs. You can also get creative to make the log pile into a design feature in your garden. There are many examples of these log pile designs on Pinterest. Even a single log dug into the ground vertically can be a benefit, especially if it is pre-drilled with a number of holes of varying sizes, as this will act as a nest home for solitary bees and a shelter for pollinating insects. If the log is placed in a sunny spot, the bees will lay their eggs in the holes and plug it up with mud and chewed leaves. Chopped logs from fallen trees can also be used to make pathway edges by laying them flat to form parallel lines to mark out a route. Insects such as ladybirds and beetles will then take up residence under the bark of these logs. Birds will also feed on the woodlice, centipedes, spiders, and worms that are attracted to the rotting wood.

A pile of stones or a dry stone wall can also provide a

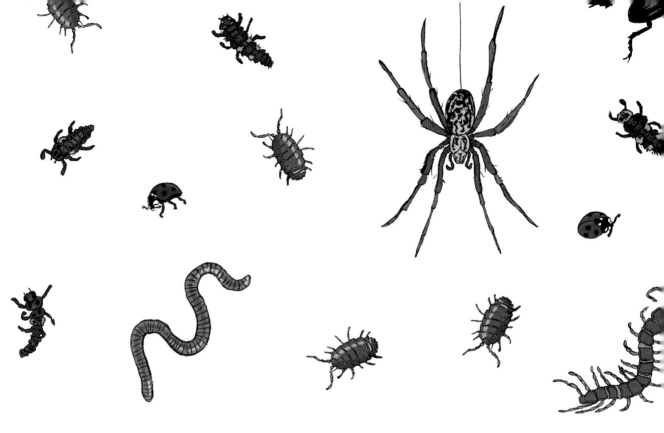

welcome habitat in your garden. Dry stone walls, traditionally built from stone with no mortar, were used to mark boundaries between fields. These attractive stone walls come in a range of shapes, sizes, colours and forms, usually constructed using local stone. The key is to have small gaps between the stones which are perfect for providing a home for a wide range of wildlife and plants in your garden. It is amazing how many species use walls in gardens. Alpine plants such as *Sempervivum*, *Saxifrage* and *Sedum* grow well in cracks and crevices. Small birds such as wrens and mammals such as field mice or voles will nest in the walls. Birds will feed off spiders and other insects living in the wall. Frogs, lizards and toads will hide in the walls and also use them as a place to bask in the sunshine. When I was a child, our dry stone wall had a family of weasels using it as their home. They used to disappear in one part of the wall and then reappear in a totally different section.

Habitat Boxes – Making Homes for Wildlife in Your Garden

One of the best ways to attract wildlife into your garden is to provide them with a home by installing a habitat box. They can be bought or made for wildlife such as hedgehogs, birds, bees, ladybirds, and bats, all of which are beneficial to your garden.

Insect Hotel

A safe and purpose-built home for insects is often referred to as an 'insect hotel'. The basic idea of an insect hotel is to use a range of different materials to create a wide variety of habitats for different insects. Generally, it is located on a south-facing post or wall (about 1 metre above the ground), and consists of a box or container stuffed full of different-sized

Insect hotels provide a variety of habitats for different insects

hollow tubes, which each have a dead end and are 10–15cm or so long. These tubes, made from bamboo, teasel stems and reeds, can provide a home for solitary bees. The container can also contain dry leaves, sticks or straw for ladybirds and lacewings. You may need to clean and maintain the hotel to reduce parasites and replace some of the materials as they rot away.

If you have more space, a large insect hotel attracting a larger range of creatures can be located on the ground using pallets. Firstly, lay some bricks on the ground as a foundation and then set 2–3 pallets on top of the bricks. Fill the gaps in the pallets to create crevices, tunnels and nests using: dead wood and loose bark; bamboo canes, sticks, stems and reeds; stones, tiles and airbricks; dry leaves, straw and corrugated cardboard. A construction of this type may also attract small mammals and amphibians as well as insects.

Bumblebee Pot/Nester

You can make a bumblebee nester using a small terracotta pot with one hole in the bottom. Fill the pot with dry leaves, straw or grass with some moss, feathers or cotton wool making up an inner core to the pot. Then find a sheltered location in the sunshine and place the pot upside down resting one edge of the pot on a slate or thin stone providing easy access for bees entering at the soil level.

Hedgehog Home

Hedgehogs are particularly good at reducing the number of slugs in your garden; however, hedgehog numbers are declining. Consider building or buying a hedgehog home. If you set it up in the spring or summer, it will be ready for the hedgehogs when they start looking for a home in the autumn prior to their winter hibernation. It is possible to find plans for making hedgehog homes on the internet but the basic principles of the design are that they have a large compartment which is insulated from the cold, with a smaller entrance corridor which will keep predators such as dogs or badgers out. It is best to locate the home in a quiet part of the garden under a hedge or behind a shed where it is out of direct sunlight with the front entrance out of the wind.

Bat Boxes

Many bats, particularly in urban areas, face problems finding suitable roosting sites. They prefer to squeeze into small warm and insulated cavities where there are few draughts. You can help them by installing a bat box and planting flowers such as night-scented stock and honeysuckle which will attract the moths and flying insects that bats like to feed on. You can make your own bat box using guidelines from the Bat Conservation Trust or buy custom-made boxes. Bat boxes should be made from rough-sawn untreated wood, as bats are sensitive to smells and preservative chemicals may be

Bat boxes can help bats to find roosting sites in built-up areas

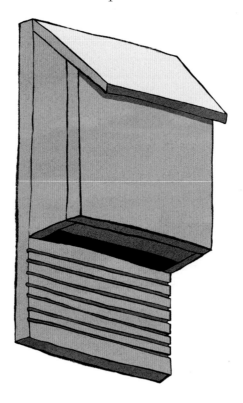

harmful to them. Generally, they have a narrow slit at the back of the box, with a rough piece of wood leading up to it that they can clamber up. Bats like to roost together, so it's a good idea to group a few of the boxes together with different sizes of slits. It is best to position your bat box on an outer wall of your house or on a tree. Choose a wall that is south facing with plenty of sun exposure. The boxes should be fixed as high up as possible, typically just below the eaves of a house roof. Ready-made boxes constructed from woodcrete (a mixture of concrete and sawdust) are among the best as they provide the greatest insulation.

Bird Boxes

Bird boxes can increase the number and species of birds in your garden. There are a wide range of designs depending on the birds you are attempting to attract. Some birds prefer open-fronted boxes, others require entrance holes of different sizes. Swallows and house martins require a cup-shaped nest under the eaves of a house. If you want to buy or build a nesting box, it is probably best to check the RSPB website to identify the most appropriate design for your box. However, there are certain general principles. Only choose a box made from an insulating material such as wood or a waterproof wood/concrete compound rather than a box made from metal or ceramics. This ensures that the box does not become too hot or too cold for chicks to survive. A box made from cedar, oak or beech will last longer than one made from a softwood such as pine. An entrance hole of around 32mm is ideal for

small birds such as sparrows and tits. Choose a smaller 28mm hole if you want to restrict the box to blue tits. Great spotted woodpeckers prey on hole-nesting birds, so to prevent this use a concrete box or fit a metal shield around the entrance hole. It is probably best to avoid a box with a perch, as they can provide assistance to weasels or squirrels attempting to reach into the box to eat eggs or chicks. Don't locate a box close to or incorporated into a bird table as the nesting birds may come into conflict with the feeding ones.

Bird Feeders

Installing bird feeders is one of the easiest ways of attracting birds to your garden. There are a wide variety of feeders available on the market. They can be made of wood and wire or plastic. It is better to use a feeder than simply scattering nuts

and scraps on the lawn as you are less likely to attract rats and mice with a feeder. If you don't want squirrels clearing out all your bird food, it may be necessary to have a squirrel-proof feeder which has a cage around the food, which stops all but the smallest birds from feeding. In terms of location, as you probably want to watch the birds, it is best to locate them in a place that is easily visible from your windows. For a very close-up view, you can even get a see-through feeder that attaches to your window with suckers. It is important to clean your feeders regularly and wash them with disinfectant to reduce the transmission of diseases among the birds.

The most common foods available for wild birds are peanuts, sunflower seeds, millet and wild bird seed mixes. In addition, freeze-dried mealworms, the larvae of the darkling beetle, are a rich source of protein. It is also possible to buy or make fat balls or cakes. These can provide high energy to birds in the winter and can be used to bind together seeds, dried fruits and mealworms. You can make fat cakes using old yogurt pots and a mixture of one part melted lard or suet with two parts seed, nuts, raisins or oats. Make a hole in the bottom of the yogurt pot and tie a piece of twine or string through the hole and up through the pot then pack the pot with your melted feed mixture. Place in the fridge overnight until the mixture hardens, cut the yogurt pot off and tie a big knot at the end of the twine to secure the food. Tie the cake in a tree or shrub then sit back and watch the birds.

Fat cakes are particularly appreciated by birds such as the robin during winte

CHAPTER 7

Wildlife and Container Ponds

*'All of a sudden I had the revelation
of how enchanting my pond was'*
CLAUDE MONET

Water for Wildlife

Of all the elements in a garden that can be created, the most effective one that encourages a wildlife sanctuary is water. Water serves so many functions: it is a place for animals to wash, drink, lay eggs and even shelter. The vast range of wildlife that benefit and rely on a source of water is immeasurable. Water in our gardens can be present in many forms from a small bird bath to a large pond. Although bird baths are good for birds, ponds really are the hub for all forms of wildlife in your garden. You may have fond childhood memories of pond dipping and seeing it teeming with life from beetle larvae to newts. For this very reason a pond is a wonderful way to engage your children with the natural world. Today, a sad figure is that 70 per cent of rural ponds in the UK have been lost over the last 100 years. Many of the remaining rural ponds are polluted from salt runoff from roads, agricultural runoff from pesticides and fertilisers leading to them being in a poor state of health. Even if your garden is a modern and contemporary design, it can greatly benefit from a wildlife pond that is well designed. Marvellously, an empty pond will develop a diverse community of life within just a few weeks.

Nymphaea (waterlily), with frog spawn

The Beneficiaries

Dragonfly, damselfly, newt, common frog, water boatman, water snail. Ponds are also a source or drinking and bathing water for a wide range of birds and mammals.

Planning Your Wildlife Pond

Choose an area of your garden, that is relatively sheltered and typically in full sun. Make sure it is not positioned directly below a deciduous tree, as the leaf fall into the pond in autumn can reduce the oxygen in the water. Think also about the likely position of large tree roots or utility pipes and cables and avoid these areas. If you are lucky enough to already have a stream in your garden, you can incorporate a pond into that water system and make it a key feature of your garden. The pond should be located where there is safe cover in terms of a hedge or long grasses for animals to retreat and hide in on the way to accessing the water. Adding a shaded area near the pond will also allow any insects or other animals an area to shelter from the sun on a hot day and prevent the water heating up too much during the summer months. Once you have selected the ideal location, mark out the pond area using canes, a hosepipe or sand. Try to keep the shape as natural as possible with few straight edges or right-angled corners. Visualise the pond layout from your house; it is often beneficial to survey the location from an upstairs window.

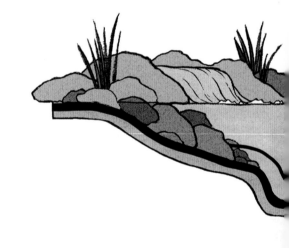

Creating Your Wildlife Pond

Excavate the soil to the depth of at least 1 metre using a spade or small digger. This depth will ensure the pond remains at a steady temperature during freezing conditions, which is essential for the species that inhabit the pond throughout the year. Make sure you leave a shallow shelf around the edges so that you can plant marginal plants. To get the best habitat possible, you should allow for at least one shallow area of the pond allowing amphibians and birds to enter and exit the water. Any soil you remove could be shaped into a banked-up area for planting a raised nectar border.

When you have finished digging the hole, check for any sharp objects or stones that could puncture a liner. Then line the hole with sand or a layer of underlay fleece. On top of this, you will install the pond liner. This is normally made of flexible PVC, EDPM rubber

A good wildlife pond will have a variety of depths combined with a bog garden to accommodate the widest range of planting

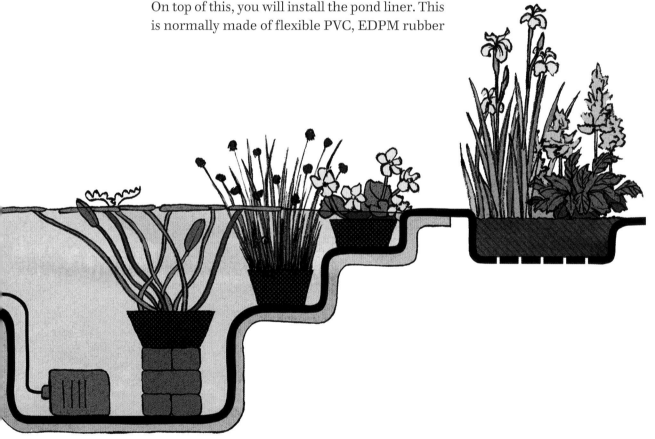

or butyl rubber. The rubber liners are more expensive than PVC but tend to last longer and are more resistant to punctures. Avoid lining a pond with concrete as it can be a nightmare if it leaks and is a fixed hard surface which can be difficult to remove in the future. Rigid pond liners, often called pre-formed pools, made of plastic or fibreglass can also be purchased from garden centres. These tend to be more suitable for small ponds and in the past, they had a reputation for only having a short lifespan. They have improved over recent years and now frequently include shelves for marginals and bog plants. They also tend to come with installation instructions. I will therefore focus on the procedure necessary for installing a pond using a flexible liner.

Roll out the liner to fully cover the hole and then from the middle of the pond take time to smooth out the liner from the deepest part to the edges with your hands. It is probably best to take off any heavy boots when you are doing this as they may damage the liner or move the underlay. If you need to fold the liner to make it fit the shape of the hole, try to make these folds as neat as you can. Then weigh down the edges with large stones and then slowly fill the liner with water to around 10cm below the soil surface. This will allow the liner to stretch to fit the contours of the hole. As the water rises, remove some of the stones to allow the liner to move fully into the pond space. Trim the edge with scissors, leaving a minimum of 15cm overlap all around the pond. Use a mixture of soil, pebbles and large stones to hold down the liner edge. A good wildlife pond will include a number of features aimed at adding wildlife to your garden. At least one side of the pond should have a shallow edge lined with pebbles or rocks. A simple wooden ramp or a pile of stones will help give any struggling swimmer a chance to get out of the water easily. This provides habitat for spawning amphibians in spring and allows visiting birds and mammals easy access without drowning. Adding a water feature and pump to keep the water moving will help keep the pond clear and healthy.

Ornamental fish should be omitted from your pond if you want to attract wildlife to your garden. Fish in your pond will eat most species they find in the water like tadpoles, water fleas and water boatman. As a result, you are unlikely to attract the full range of insects, amphibians, birds and mammals.

You can also incorporate a small bog garden at the edge of the pond. A bog garden is simply an area of soil that is constantly damp. It should not be waterlogged, instead it should be an area that is slow draining. It can be created by laying a liner in a hollow next to the pond with a small number of drainage holes (one to two 1cm holes every square metre). Add a thin layer of grit or gravel on the liner and then top up the rest of the hollow with a mix of 3 parts of compost, 3 parts of topsoil and 1 part grit. You will need to water the bog garden regularly during dry periods in spring and summer.

Pond Plants

Pond plants provide a habitat for wildlife like tadpoles, newts, dragonflies and pond snails. It is best to design your pond planting with a good combination of submerged, floating and marginal plants, as each one will provide specific habitat for wildlife to establish. Marginal plants can be planted into baskets topped with gravel and placed on the edges with the floating and submerged plants placed into the deeper water. Ideally, you want to focus on planting native plants – this means they have no way of causing damage to the natural environment or waterways if they escape the pond location. For example, American skunk cabbage (*Lysichiton americanus*), which was planted in ornamental ponds in the 19th and 20th centuries, has now become an invasive species across many waterways in the UK, choking out many natural riverside ecosystems. Water-based invasive species are far more difficult to control as seed can travel in the water and whole waterways can be taken over by the plants.

All ponds should have oxygenator plants. These plants, which play the vital role in keeping the water oxygenated, have their leaves submerged in the water. By providing oxygen to the water, they will allow the reptile, amphibian and insect species of the pond to thrive. They are also good at keeping the water clear by absorbing both the minerals and carbon dioxide that support algae. They are nearly always sold in bunches held together by a weight. Although they could be just dropped in the water, it is probably best to plant them in a shallow basket of gravel and place the basket at the bottom of the pond in late spring. Some examples of oxygenator plants are:

Ceratophyllum demersum (hornwort)
    A submerged aquatic plant with forked, dark green leaves and tiny flowers in summer
Marsilea quadrifolia (European water clover)
    A spreading aquatic plant with dark green leaves formed of 4 triangular leaflets

Ceratophyllum demersum (hornwort)

Ranunculus aquatilis (common water crowfoot)
     A short-lived aquatic plant with thread-like submerged leaves and lobed floating leaves with solitary white flowers in summer

DEEP WATER PLANTS

Deep water plants can survive right in the middle of the pond, producing foliage which floats on the water surface. Probably the most popular are the charming and beautiful waterlilies (*Nymphaea*). When it comes to these plants, make sure you research their preferred depth of water before planting in a pond. Plant in open-sided containers in late spring and summer using heavy loam or aquatic compost with a thin layer of gravel on top. Introduce the plants to the pond gradually, lowering the basket until it finally rests on the bottom of the pond after a few weeks. The aim should be to stand the basket on a few bricks so that the crown of the plant is around 10cm below the surface. Then remove the bricks in response to growth in the plant until it eventually reaches its permanent position on the bottom of the pond. To successfully grow waterlilies, you need calm, still water away from disturbance by waterfalls, fountains or pumps. They are best planted in an open position with full sun, and can benefit from a supplementary feed with a specialist aquatic plant food to encourage better flowering.

Aponogeton distachyos (water hyacinth)
     Submerged aquatic plant with floating leaves and small, white flowers held just above the water surface
Callitriche palustris (water starwort)
     Submerged aquatic plant that spreads to the surface forming mats of densely packed small green leaves on the surface. Gives good surface cover and produces tiny white flowers during summer
Hydrocharis morsus-ranae (frogbit)
     Submerged aquatic plant that spreads to the surface with floating glossy, rounded leaves and white, 3-petalled flowers in summer

Nymphaea (waterlily)

Nymphaea (waterlily)
    Submerged aquatic plant with floating, rounded leaves
    and showy bowl-shaped flowers in a wide range of colours
    on the water surface, followed by submerged, berry-like
    fruits

Stratiotes aloides (water soldier)
    Submerged aquatic plant with stalkless rosettes of toothed,
    sword-shaped leaves, and white or pinkish flowers in
    summer

MARGINAL PLANTS

This set of plants are found situated around the edge of your
pond in the shallow water. They have their roots submerged
and their leaves and flowers above the surface of the water.
They are planted for their interesting leaves and floral colour,
but also help to aesthetically soften the edges of the pond.
They can be grown in soil on the marginal shelf of the pond,
but are probably best set into baskets similar to the deep-
water plants, aquatic pots or planted straight into the soil.
Some noteworthy plants found in this group are:

Caltha palustris (marsh marigold)
> A marsh plant with heart-shaped leaves and cup-shaped yellow or white flowers in early spring

Carex elata (tufted sedge)
> An evergreen plant with upright or arching, narrow, bright yellow leaves and short or long spikes of tiny green or brown flowers in early summer

Eriophorum angustifolium (common cotton grass)
> An evergreen plant with linear leaves, black-scaled, silky-haired flower heads, followed by cottony white fruiting heads

Iris pseudacorus (yellow flag)
> A plant with narrow, erect foliage and branched stems bearing several yellow flowers in June/July

Iris versicolor (blue flag)
> A plant with narrow, erect foliage and branched stems bearing several bluish-purple flowers in spring or early summer

Juncus ensifolius (swordleaf rush)
> A species of rush with flat but curving leaves with dark brown to black tips

Caltha palustris
(marsh marigold)

Menyanthes trifoliata (bogbean)
> Forms wide mats with leaves held just above the water, and pale pink star-shaped flowers with fringed petals in summer

Myosotis scorpioides (water forget-me-not)
> A plant with small leaves and clusters of small, salver-shaped blue, yellow or white flowers in spring or early summer

Pontederia cordata (pickerel weed)
> Marginal aquatic plant forming clumps of erect, linear leaves with spikes of blue flowers in late summer and early autumn

Veronica beccabunga (water pimpernel)
> Marginal, evergreen aquatic plant with creeping hollow stems with fleshy leaves. Spikes of small, bright blue flowers are produced in late spring to late summer

BOG PLANTS

These plants are located in the bog garden constructed at the side of the pond. They require damp humus-rich soil which is neither waterlogged nor allowed to fully dry out. They should be planted in a similar fashion to plants in a normal border. They can be very attractive both in terms of architectural foliage and flowers.

Astilbe
> A plant with shiny, dark green, divided foliage and dark red stems and erect clusters of tiny white, pink or purple flowers in summer

Darmera peltata (umbrella plant)
> A vigorous plant forming an extensive clump of long-stalked, large glossy leaves that turn red in autumn. Clusters of pale pink star-shaped flowers arise on tall stems before the leaves

Iris pseudacorus (yellow flag)
> A plant which can be both a marginal and bog plant, it has narrow, erect foliage and branched stems bearing several yellow flowers in June/July

Iris versicolor (blue flag)

A plant which can be both a marginal and bog plant, it has narrow, erect foliage and branched stems bearing several bluish-purple flowers in spring or early summer

Persicaria (knotweed)

A sub-shrub with large, pointed, oval leaves and spikes of bell-shaped white or pink flowers in mid-summer to autumn

Primula candelabra hybrids

A moisture-loving plant forming a rosette of leaves with erect stems of bell-shaped pink, red, purple, yellow, orange, or white flowers in late spring and early summer

Primula florindae (Tibetan cowslip)

Erect stems with broad leaves carrying bunches of nodding yellow flowers in summer

Rheum palmatum (ornamental rhubarb)

A robust plant with very large leaves and tall leafy stems bearing large clusters of tiny flowers

Rodgersia

A moisture-loving plant with strongly veined leaves and clusters of small white or pink flowers in summer

Pond Maintenance

It is particularly important to look after your pond by tidying and thinning out the plants every couple of years, as many aquatic pond plants can spread and take over the water area if you do not keep them in check. The best time to clean your pond is in late autumn when many creatures are less active. Generally, you want to maintain at least one third of the water surface visible for wildlife. It is also important to note that when you clear out your pond you should make sure that you leave any waste material on the side of the pond for a few days to allow any tiny creatures to slip safely back into the water. You should scoop out any excess silt from the base of the pond and this can be used on your plant borders. In late spring and early summer, pond algae and weed growth can be a problem for ponds. If you have a small pond, you can add barley straw to the water to reduce the blanket weed and algae growth. There are various ways of controlling and preventing these problems. Blanket weed can be easily removed by twisting it around a stick, but you will have to keep doing this on a regular basis. Alternatively, you can float a mesh bag of barley straw on the pond at a concentration of around 50g per square metre. If you add the straw in the early spring, it should work for around six months, and you need to remove it when it turns black. Pond dye can also be considered as a way of preventing algae. It works by colouring the water with black vegetable dye, making it difficult for the algae to photosynthesise. This can make the pond look quite attractive, but you should make sure your deep-water plants have their leaves on the surface before putting the dye in the pond.

Container Ponds for Smaller Gardens or Patios

Not everyone has the space for a normal pond, and it may be daunting to undertake the excavation necessary for a garden pond. An alternative is to create a pond in a container. This can be located on a patio or balcony, and can be taken with

you if you move to a new house. To create a container pond, you firstly need to find a suitable container. This could be an old tin bath, a whisky barrel, a Belfast sink or an agricultural water trough. The only conditions are that it has a depth of at least 30–40cm and it is watertight. If there are leaks, you could use a piece of flexible pond liner inside the container. The container pond can be placed in a shady or sunny location. Similar if somewhat smaller plants can be placed in a container in the same manner as would be done in a large pond. There should be a balance of oxygenators, emergent vegetation, and flowering plants. It is important to try to leave some area of open water, as this will allow dragonflies and damselflies to lay their eggs. It is best to use rainwater to fill and maintain the levels in the container pond, but if you can't, use tap water and allow it to sit aside for a few days to enable the chlorine to evaporate before adding the water to the pond.

Container ponds can provide a good habitat for wildlife in your garden, including common frogs, newts, and some dragonflies. If you want to attract amphibians such as frogs and newts, it is best to create easy access by adding some form of 'frog ladder' (piles of wood or stones arranged next to the container).

Dragonflies thrive around container ponds and other water features

CHAPTER 8

Creating a Rain Garden and Water Management

'The best thing to do when it's raining is to let it rain'
HENRY WADSWORTH LONGFELLOW

Climate change can result in a significant change in rainfall patterns with many parts of the UK receiving a mixture of heavy rain downpours and episodes of drought. The periods of heavy rain can result in flash flooding, and for some people creating a rain garden may be even more important than incorporating a pond into their garden. The problem can be exacerbated by the growth in the use of hard landscaping such as tarmac, concrete or monoblock driveways. All of these can stop water from slowly soaking away after a storm. Instead, there is runoff from the hard surfaces which can lead to waterlogging of borders and lawns or flooding in streets and houses.

In the Royal Botanic Garden Edinburgh, heavy rainfall events have brought problems of waterlogging and localised flooding to some parts of the Garden, causing damage to plant beds, lawns and footpaths, and impacting on visitor access due to the closure of affected areas. To address this, a rain garden was planted in one part of the Garden, and as a result when heavy rain falls, it successfully absorbs the excess water and reduces flooding on nearby paths. A campaign to encourage householders and businesses to install rain gardens to help reduce flooding has also been launched by the Scottish Green Infrastructure Forum (SGIF).

A rain garden is an area of vegetation that catches rainwater and then releases it very slowly, which helps reduce the severity and likelihood of flooding. With extreme weather events expected to become more frequent and intense over the coming decades, rain gardens may become a necessity. Rain gardens help reduce pollution by filtering out contaminants collected in water runoff before it enters streams and rivers. They can also help filter air, provide habitats for wildlife and reduce noise pollution.

The Beneficiaries

Bee, butterfly, common frog, moth, ladybird, lacewing, spider, beetle, hoverfly, bat, song thrush, goldfinch, chaffinch, blue tit, great tit.

Creating a Rain Garden

Rain garden – a shallow basin with vegetation designed to encourage water to drain naturally into the ground or get taken up by plants

A rain garden is designed as a shallow basin with absorbent yet free-draining soil, and planted with vegetation that can withstand occasional drought and flooding. The design is aimed at encouraging water to drain naturally into the ground, or get taken up by the plants and lost to the air by evapotranspiration. In terms of soil, the best mix is around

30 per cent existing soil, 45 per cent sand, 10 per cent gravel and 15 per cent compost.

The plants introduced into this soil are an important part of its functionality, largely affecting its efficiency in terms of rainwater absorption. They tend to be far more efficient than lawns at soaking up or trapping excess rainfall. The plants aid rainwater runoff management by improving soil infiltration, water retention in the root zone, and enhancing evaporation and transpiration via the vegetation. They also tend to be good at providing nectar sources for insects, food for seed-eating birds and habitats for invertebrates. The ideal plants are:

NATIVE PLANTS

Anthyllis vulneraria (kidney vetch)
An open grassland plant that has feather-like leaves and clusters of small pea-like yellow to red flowers in summer

Cicerbita alpina (alpine sowthistle)

    An upland plant with tall unbranched stems with blue-violet 'dandelion' flowers in summer

Filipendula ulmaria (meadowsweet)

    A vigorous plant with feather-type leaves and sprays of small rosy pink or white flowers on leafy stems set above the foliage in summer

Knautia arvensis (field scabious)

    A clump-forming plant with feather-type leaves and lilac-blue flowers in summer and autumn

Saxifraga granulata (meadow saxifrage)

    Mat-forming plant with kidney shaped, glossy leaves and upright stems with rounded, white flowers in late spring

Succisa pratensis (blue bonnets)

    A plant with a rosette of leaves and long-stalked, solitary pale violet, pincushion-like flowers in late summer and autumn

NON-NATIVE PLANTS

Aquilegia formosa (columbine)

    A clump-forming plant with long-stalked leaves and erect, leafy stems with bell-shaped red-orange flowers from May to August

Aruncus dioicus (goat's beard)

    A clump-forming plant with broad, light-green leaves and arching tiny creamy- white flowers in summer

Hosta sieboldiana (Siebold's plantain lily)

    A clump-forming plant with broad blue-green leaves and white, bell-shaped flowers, held on stems in summer

Ligularia fischeri (Fischer's leopard plant)

A robust clump-forming plant with coarsely toothed light-green leaves and clusters of yellow or orange, daisy-like flower heads in summer followed by brown or purple seeds

Primula poissonii (Poisson's primrose)

A semi-evergreen plant with a rosette of leaves with erect stems carrying reddish-purple flowers in summer

Plants are generally selected that are known to thrive in wet conditions; however, levels of moisture can vary in a rain garden from very wet in the centre to very dry at the edge. Plants such as *Filipendula ulmaria*, *Cicerbita alpina*, *Ligularia fischeri* and *Aruncus dioicus* are probably more suited to the centre, with *Aquilegia formosa* and *Anthyllis vulneriana* being more suited to the drier edges. Once planted, a layer of gravel and organic mulch should be spread over the area. This layer will help to retain soil moisture during dry periods, whilst also helping to stop erosion of the soil and reduce maintenance by suppressing weeds.

As there is no open bare soil, the rain garden is relatively easy to maintain once the vegetation cover is established. The herbaceous perennials in the planting need to be cut back in winter and early spring, and only in exceptionally dry conditions will the area require any watering. Although the deciduous plants which die back in the winter will contribute almost

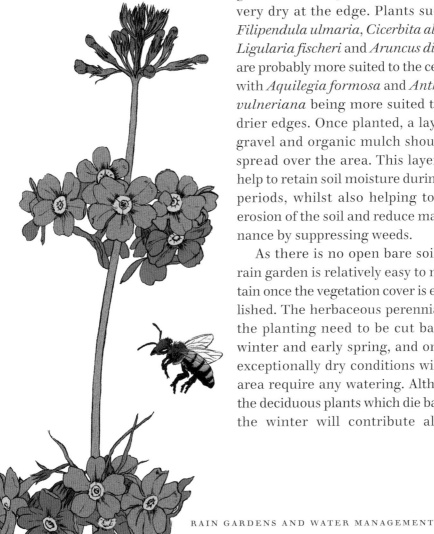

nothing to evapotranspiration during the winter, these types of plants will still take up water in winter months via their root system.

Water Management

Your garden may also experience lengthy periods of dry weather, so care needs to be taken in ensuring that we use water wisely. Frequently, local authorities will impose hosepipe bans and at all times gardeners should be trying to do their best to minimise their use of tap water. The most effective way to reduce the use of mains water in your garden is to collect and store rainwater in water butts. Rainwater is often better for your plants than tap water, for example with ericaceous plants such as azaleas, as it often has a lower pH. The minerals that are sometimes found in mains water, particularly in hard-water areas, can raise the pH of the root zone, affecting the nutrient availability. Connecting a water butt to a gutter downpipe from a greenhouse, shed, garage or house can be used to collect the rainwater. If the butt has a tap at the base and sits on a stand it is much easier to access the water with your watering can. The butt should also have a lid to stop wildlife falling in and prevent algal growth.

In addition to using rainwater, you can also recycle and use grey water from baths, showers and washing up in your garden. However, it is advisable that grey water from your home should not be used for watering food crops, but is generally suitable for all other types of plants.

It is possible to maximize any water you do use by only watering in the cool of the morning or evening rather than in the heat of the day when water will quickly evaporate. A good depth of mulch on your borders such as manure or wood chips will help retain moisture in the soil for a much longer period of time and reduce the amount of watering required. When planting woody plants or trees, it is often best to create a soil dam around the plant at about 30cm from it. This can be filled with water. If this is done slowly, the water should not erode the soil dam. Doing this not only gets the water to where it needs to be, but also reduces the amount of water used. Finally, water can be saved by making sure there are no leaks in your hoses or water butts.

To improve drainage in the garden, there are things that can be done to reduce the impact of paths and hard landscaping. If you have a paved path, don't repoint your path, plant in the gaps instead. The plants will eventually knit together and will out-compete any weeds. Some suggested plants are thyme (*Thymus serpyllum*), Corsican mint (*Mentha requienii*), heath pearlwort (*Sagina subulata*) or Mexican fleablane (*Erigeron karvinskianus*). This will not only allow water to drain away between the paving slabs, but will also attract pollinators. Some of these plants will even emit a fragrance when they are walked on. To plant in these gaps, use a soil knife or weeding knife to scrape out joints and create a planting pocket. Then use a planting mix of one part sand and three parts multi-purpose peat-free compost for planting. Alternatively, you can create a path of stepping-stones with wider areas of planting between the stones. Even in driveways for cars you can incorporate a planting space to help biodiversity by planting a strip down the middle of the driveway. Cellular grids made from plastic or concrete grids will allow you to park a car on grass whilst allowing the grass to grow and water runoff to drain away.

When establishing new paths, it is worthwhile adopting alternative paving materials that are permeable and allow water to drain into the soil. Permeable block paving laid on grit has porous gaps that allow rainwater to pass through it and back into the soil below, preventing runoff. Gravel, grass and wood chips can be used to create free-draining paths. Tree surgeons usually have a big supply of wood chip and are often willing to drop some off for your garden for free. Finally, a more expensive option is to use resin-bonded gravel, a long-lasting solution, which allows water to pass through the layers into the ground.

CHAPTER 9

Combining Nature with Fruit and Vegetable Production

'A vegetable garden doesn't just feed your body.
It also feeds your soul'
DOUG GREEN

In the past, fruit and vegetables in our gardens were grown out of necessity to feed the household. Today, supermarkets ensure that these items are widely available and reasonably affordable. However, there is nothing more enjoyable than harvesting super-fresh fruit and vegetables that you have cosseted and cared for in your own garden.

As there are many books that focus in detail on the selection, growing and harvesting of every form of fruit and vegetable, this chapter focuses instead on the issues involved in maintaining a fruit and vegetable patch in a garden that is designed to invite wildlife.

It is a common misconception that a garden which is aimed at attracting nature is a difficult garden environment for successful fruit and vegetable cultivation. It is true that many insects, birds and other animals are as attracted to tasty fruit and vegetables as we are, but there are natural ways that we can protect our harvest without resorting to chemicals. Whatever fruit and vegetables are being cultivated, there are three broad approaches to protecting the plants and the anticipated harvest without adversely impacting on the natural balance of the garden. These are defensive barriers, companion planting and nematodes.

Defensive Barriers

Defensive barriers can be particularly effective in protecting soft fruit and vegetables from birds, rabbits, slugs and snails. A well-built fruit cage constructed of poles and nets, or simply nets placed over individual fruit bushes, can deter birds from eating the ripe fruit or even the flowers which will eventually form the fruit. Similarly, nets can be used to keep pigeons off brassicas such as cauliflowers, cabbages, broccoli, turnips and Brussels sprouts. Alternatively, bamboo cloches can be used to protect individual brassicas from birds. Some gardeners hang aluminium foil or old CDs from strings over their vegetables to deter birds, but often the effectiveness of these tends to be short lived. Models of predator birds such as hawks can also be useful, particularly if they move in the wind. These models do not need to be too lifelike, and can simply be a V shape cut out of cardboard or a potato with a few feathers sticking out of it.

Netting can also be used to deter the cabbage white butterfly laying its eggs on brassicas. The butterfly itself isn't the

Nets are a useful way of protecting vegetables and soft fruit, particularly from birds

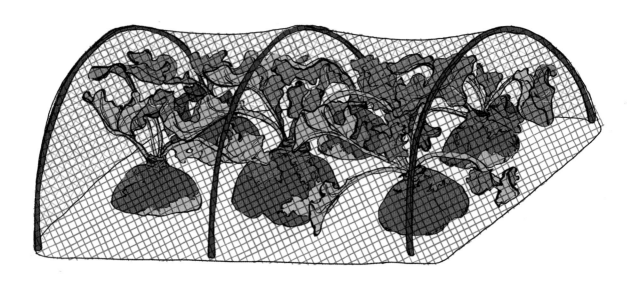

problem, it is the resultant caterpillars which can devastate a crop. To deter the butterflies, finer netting than that used for birds can be draped over the young plants, or it may be possible to use some of the companion planting methods mentioned later in this chapter.

Building a defensive barrier against rabbits is more difficult, although some gardeners attempt to deter them by constructing a fence made of hazel twigs around the vegetable bed. Alternatively, growing the vegetables or fruit such as strawberries in raised beds may keep all but the most athletic rabbits at bay.

Defensive barriers can also be used to deter slugs and snails. Copper ring barriers around plants can repel the most enthusiastic mollusc. However, they tend to be expensive. Alternatives could be created by snipping aluminium drinks cans into rings with a spiky rim and placing these around the plants. Slugs and snails do not like crossing very rough surfaces, so surrounding plants with crushed seashells, crushed cocoa shells, egg shells, ashes or coffee grounds may also be effective. However, these need to be replenished regularly since birds and rain can disturb them.

Companion Planting

Defensive barriers are of little use in protecting against the many smaller creatures feasting on fruit and vegetable crops. Companion planting can be used as a natural way of deterring such creatures. For example, planting aromatic herbs (lemon balm, sage, oregano, borage, dill, rosemary) and/or high-blossom flowers (French marigold, calendula, nasturtium) near or among brassicas can keep the cabbage white butterfly away. Similarly, these plants can also be used to disguise other fruit and vegetables hidden among them from aphids, whiteflies, carrot flies and other pests which hunt by smell.

Companion plants can also be used to attract beneficial insects which prey on particular pests. Many of these highly

scented plants, such as the poached egg plant (*Limnanthes douglasii*), wormwood (*Artemisia absinthium*) or marigold (*Calendula officinalis*), attract hoverflies, lacewings and ladybirds, which eat aphids.

VALUABLE COMPANION PLANTS

Allium tuberosum (garlic chive)
*Artemisia absinthium (*wormwood)
Borago officinalis (borage)
Calendula officinalis (marigold)
Foeniculum vulgare (fennel)
Lavandula angustifolia (English lavender)
Mentha spicata (mint)
Salvia officinalis (sage)
Thymus vulgaris (thyme)
Tropaeolum majus (nasturtium)

Nematodes

Nematodes can also be used to defend against beetles, slugs, caterpillars, vine weevils, cutworms, chafers, ants, leatherjackets, whiteflies, grubs, and thrips. Nematodes are microscopic worms that infect the target pest. These nematodes can be purchased from garden centres or specialist organic garden supply companies. They are then mixed with water and applied using a watering can to the area requiring protection. It is also possible to get a prepared mix of nematode species for fruit and vegetables which targets a broad range of pests with one application, combatting carrot root fly, cabbage root fly, leatherjackets, cutworms, onion fly, sciarid fly, caterpillars, gooseberry sawfly, thrips and codling moth. As the nematodes are live material, they have to be used within two to three weeks of purchase. A nematode application usually lasts around 6 weeks in the soil, and it is harmless to children, pets and wildlife.

Let Nature Take Control

If you have developed a garden that attracts nature, then the natural world itself may help to protect your fruit and vegetables. Frogs, newts, toads, hedgehogs, and birds such as thrushes will help to control the numbers of slugs and snails. Blue tits, wrens, wasps, ladybirds, lacewings and hoverflies will control aphids. Owls and foxes may control the populations of mice and rabbits whilst many birds will eat caterpillars and various insects. Creating a true ecosystem within the garden should hopefully stop any one species getting out of control and ultimately protect your harvest.

Lavandula angustifolia
(English lavender)

CHAPTER 10

Creating Green Roofs and Living Walls

'The sky's the limit if you have a roof over your head'
SOL HUROK

Greening ordinary outbuildings in your garden like your garage or shed can enhance the environment for wildlife in your garden. Rather than trying to hide or screen a shed or garage, why not make them a garden feature by adding a green roof? A green roof is simply adding a growing substrate and plants to a roof. This will soften any built structure and, once it has been installed, it can provide habitats and food sources for a range of insects and birds, cut carbon emissions and reduce water runoff hugely. You can even think outside the box and cover your bin store or bird boxes with a green roof.

Rooftops can be a difficult environment for plants to grow and establish. For this reason, it is essential that the correct plants are selected for the conditions. The plants need to be low maintenance and able to cope with drought, elevated temperatures, and wind exposure. The shallow soil substrate on roofs certainly limits the plants' ability to survive through drought, but deeper amounts of soil are often not possible because of the weight-bearing limits on the roofs of structures and buildings.

Commonly, green roofs in the UK are planted with sedums or other low-growing succulents. You can even buy ready prepared sedum matting to put on a roof. Why not try an edible roof? It is even possible to grow herbs or even strawberries on top of your shed in an easily reached location.

The Beneficiaries

Bee, butterfly, moth, spider, blue tit, great tit.

How to Make a Green Roof

Make sure before you start that the roof is strong enough to support a green roof. In some cases, you may need to add additional supports to strengthen the roof so that it can withstand the additional weight. Ideally you need a roof that has a slope as a flat surface is more likely to get waterlogged. The slope shouldn't be too steep, or everything may slide down the roof, but a pitch of between 3 and 15 degrees is probably ideal. The first step is to build a box-shaped frame to fit the size of your roof. This will be around 10–15cm in depth in order to hold the growing media for the plants. Generally, this will be made out of treated wood, but could also be made of metal. Drainage

A frame to hold the growing media on a green roof showing:

1 waterproof liner
2 drainage holes
3 grid of wooden cells
4 free-draining base layer
5 top-layer of loam-based compost and grit
6 small planting holes
7 planting of succulents, sedges and grasses
8 plants fill gaps as they become established

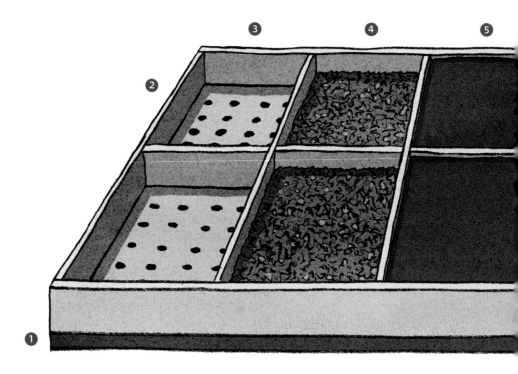

holes every 5–10cm should be made in the frame at the bottom of any slope to let excess water escape. If the roof area is large, it is advisable to divide the frame into a grid of wooden cells.

Even if the shed or garage roof is waterproof, it is still advisable to put a liner, such as a flexible pond liner, on the shed before securely fastening the frame to the roof with screws. Once the frame has been installed you can add a free-draining material such as crushed brick, gravel or vermiculite at about 6cm depth. Top up the remaining space with a free-draining mix of loam-based compost and grit. It is then possible to proceed with planting the succulents or possibly grasses and sedges using a trowel to create small holes in the planting material. Alternatively, if sedum matting is used, it can be rolled out on the roof in a similar manner to the rolling out of turf on a lawn. It is important to make sure no gaps are left between the mats. Water the plants in until they become established.

Roof Plants

ALPINES AND SUCCULENTS

Anemone nemorosa (wood anemone)
Mat-forming plant with divided leaves and rosette-like green flowers in spring. Grows to height of around 15cm.

Aquilegia bertolonii (Bertoloni columbine)
A clump-forming plant with leafy stems bearing bell-shaped violet-blue flowers in late spring/early summer. Grows to height of 30cm.

Haberlea rhodopensis (rhodope haberlea)
A clump-forming evergreen plant with a rosette of hairy, dark green leaves and funnel-shaped violet flowers marked orange on the white throat in spring and early summer. Grows to height of 15cm.

Saxifraga x urbium (London pride)
An evergreen mat-forming plant producing rosettes of spoon-shaped, long-stalked leaves and small pink-white flowers from early summer. Grows to 30cm in height.

Sedum acre/Sedum rupestre/Sedum album (stonecrop)
A mat-forming, evergreen plant with small, fleshy leaves and yellow or white star-shaped flowers from May to July. Grows to 10cm in height.

Saxifraga urbium
(London pride)

Sempervivum caucasicum (houseleek)

An evergreen mat-forming plant with rosettes of fleshy green leaves with reddish-brown tips and star-shaped pink or pale-yellow flowers appearing on stems in summer. Grows to 20cm in height.

GRASSES AND SEDGES

Carex testacea (orange New Zealand sedge)

An evergreen sedge with narrow, olive-green arching leaves in summer, the colour intensifying to warm coppery-orange in winter. Spikes of tiny green or brown flowers. Grows to 40cm in height.

Festuca glauca 'Blaufuchs' (blue fescue)

An evergreen grass with linear ice-blue leaves, becoming greener in winter. In late spring/summer it has blue-green flower plumes that turn golden-brown. Grows to 30cm in height.

Sempervivum caucasicum (houseleek)

Poa labillardierei (New Zealand blue grass)
> A semi-evergreen grass with slender blue-green leaves to 50–60cm long, with sprays of purplish flowers above the foliage in midsummer.

Stipa tenuissima (Mexican feather grass)
> A deciduous grass with thread-like leaves and arching clusters of green/brown flowers in summer.

Like most gardens, there is no such thing as maintenance-free planting. However, where possible, green roofs have been designed to be as low maintenance as possible. At least once a year, it is best to remove any weeds, seedlings and accumulated leaf litter that may have come from nearby trees. Grasses and sedges may also need a trim annually to stop them from getting out of hand. Two years after a green roof has been established, an application of a slow-release granular fertiliser should be provided. Vegetation mats with a mix composed mainly of Sedum on thin substrates may need feeding more often (once or twice a year).

It is important to fill any bare patches that appear in the planting as this will stop weeds becoming established on your roof. Also check the drainage holes regularly to ensure they are clear. There are few pest or disease problems with green roofs, but it is important to always remain vigilant and spot anything early before it can spread and become a serious issue.

On a much smaller scale, a green roof can also be grown on a bird house. This follows the same principles as the larger green roofs. A 4cm frame is built on top of and around the roof of the bird house. A waterproof liner is attached to the roof and then the frame is filled with moist potting compost. Cover the compost with moist sphagnum moss and hold this in place by stapling chicken wire over the moss onto the frame, ensuring that there are no sharp edges left on the wire. Push even more sphagnum moss through the mesh to fill any gaps until you cannot see the compost underneath. Finally, plant sedums by pushing them into the moss with your fingers or a screwdriver.

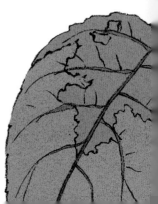

Living Walls

Living or green walls can provide habitats for insects and birds, as well as offering great aesthetic benefits. They can cover up an unattractive building façade or boundary wall. A living wall can simply consist of climbing plants growing naturally or supported by trellises or wires. The most appropriate plants are climbers, wall shrubs or apple or pear trees trained as espaliers or fans. Alternatively, it is possible to purchase living wall systems which can range from fabric grow bags that you can hang on the wall, a plastic cell-like structure with pockets containing compost, or other growing media which are connected to drip irrigation. Small plug plants, not necessarily climbers, are also suitable.

CLIMBERS FOR A SUNNY SOUTH OR WEST-FACING WALL

Actinidia kolomikta

Vigorous, deciduous climber with white flowers and attractive leaves tipped with silver, later pink; height 4–8m; flowers in summer; prefers full sun on well-drained moist soil.

Actinidia kolomikta

Clematis
Many varieties in colours including pinks, purples and whites; height 1–3m; flowers dependant on the variety in spring, summer or autumn; prefers full sun or partial shade on well-drained moist soil.

Lonicera sempervirens (trumpet honeysuckle)
Blue-green leaves with orange-red flowers followed by red berries; height 2–4m; flowers spring–autumn; prefers full sun or partial shade on well-drained moist soil.

Trachelospermum (jasmine)
An evergreen climbing shrub with glossy leaves and clusters of star-shaped highly fragrant flowers; height 2–4m; flowers in summer; prefers full sun or partial shade on well-drained moist soil.

Lonicera sempervirens (trumpet honeysuckle)

Wisteria

A vigorous deciduous woody climber with green leaves and clusters of fragrant, pea-like, violet-blue, white or pink flowers; height 4–8m; flowers in summer; prefers full sun or partial shade on well-drained moist soil.

CLIMBERS FOR A SHADY NORTH OR EAST-FACING WALL

Akebia quinata (chocolate vine)

A vigorous semi-evergreen climber with bright green leaves and fragrant reddish-purple flowers, followed by purple, sausage-shaped fruits; height 8–12m; flowers in summer; prefers full sun or partial shade on well-drained moist soil.

Garrya elliptica (silk tassel bush)

A vigorous evergreen plant with leathery leaves and small greenish flowers in catkin-like clusters; height 2–4m; flowers in spring; prefers full sun or partial shade on well-drained soil.

Hydrangea anomala

A vigorous, deciduous climber with green leaves. Flowers can be white, pink or pale red; height 8–12m; flowers in summer; prefers partial shade on well-drained soil.

Parthenocissus (Virginia creeper)

A vigorous deciduous climber with leaves that have an attractive orange-red autumn colour; very small green flowers followed by blue or black berries; height 8–12m; flowers in summer; prefers full shade or partial shade on well-drained moist soil.

Rosa (climbing rose)

Many varieties of climbing rose in a variety of colours of solitary or clustered flowers; height 1.5–3m; flowers in summer; prefers full sun or partial shade on well-drained moist soil.

CHAPTER 11

Producing Valuable Compost

'Nature is a totally efficient, self-regenerating system.
If we discover the laws that govern this system and live
synergistically within them, sustainability will follow'
R. BUCKMINSTER FULLER

Soil

The very basis of UK soil is made up of three components: clay, sand, and silt. These are inorganic particles. Clay has the smallest particles, sand has the largest, and silt sits between the two. The ratio of the components will determine what type of soil you have. You can do a simple soil test by rubbing soil from your garden into a sausage shape in the palm of your hand and if it stays in that shape, it is most likely that your soil is made up of a higher proportion of clay particles. Clay soil is typically fertile but tends to be wetter and is prone to waterlogging. Sandy soil, on the other hand, will not bind together when wet and will be very free draining with poor mineral content. A silt soil is somewhere in between as it will retain some water, but can become easily compacted.

A fertile soil is full of decaying plant material and healthy beneficial organisms. It tends to be a complex ecosystem composed of microbes, invertebrates, insects, worms, nematodes, roots, fungi, algae and spores. This ecosystem relies on a regular supply of organic matter. How do you source this bulky organic matter for your garden? The answer is to make your own compost. Whatever size of garden you have, large or small, you can make your own compost which is the cheapest soil improver available.

The Beneficiaries

Woodlice, centipedes, millipedes, beetles, worms, toads, slow worms, grass snakes.

Making Compost

When making compost, you are trying to speed up and replicate the process of organic matter decomposition that occurs in the soil. This can be done by creating a heap of rotting organic matter or by placing the material in a compost bin. The decomposition tends to be quicker and tidier in a compost bin as it retains warmth and moisture. The bigger the bin, the more efficient the process. One cubic metre has always been recommended as a minimum for fast, hot composting. The most common type of compost bin is a four-sided wooden container that can be accessed from a front panel. They can be purchased or made from wooden battens, old floorboards or old wooden pallets. A compost container can take quite a battering and a full load of compost is quite a weight, so make sure it is sturdy. The container is open to the soil at the bottom to enable good drainage and easy ingress for worms and other creatures that are important in the composting process. It should also be covered with a lid, tarpaulin, or old carpet to retain the heat. It should have few, if any, holes or gaps in the sides as this can result in the compost drying and heat escaping. To be most efficient in making compost, it is best to have two containers, one that can be left to rot while the other is filled up.

It is also possible to buy plastic compost bins, although these sometimes result in the compost getting either too wet or too dry, whereas a wooden bin allows the compost to breathe and also provides a reasonable level of insulation. They are, however, potentially more suitable for a relatively small garden or where the compost bin can be viewed from the house.

A compost tumbler is a barrel-shaped container in a metal framework that can be rotated by hand. The container is filled with the same ingredients as a normal compost bin, left for a few days to allow the composting to start, and then turned several times each week. The turning action of the tumbler ensures that all the contents are well composted. A tumbler has the added benefit of being vermin-proof. Compost tumblers tend to heat up very well, and after three to four weeks will produce a reasonable compost. To function properly, the tumbler needs to be filled all at once, so is not suitable for adding material a little at a time. It also requires a strong arm and hard work as it takes a lot of effort to turn a full tumbler.

There are also hot composting bins which are insulated boxes (wheelie bin size) with a close-fitting lid. They sometimes have built-in carbon filters to absorb any smells, a temperature gauge and a tank in the base to collect the liquid produced during composting. They are designed to allow decomposition at a much higher temperature and a higher speed and result in a finer compost. However, they tend to be more expensive than the other types of bin.

The end goal of any compost bin is to deliver a large quantity of brown, crumbly, sweet-smelling compost which you can use to improve your soil and in turn provide nutrients to feed your plants. To achieve this, you need to add the correct type of materials. Generally, any soft garden waste is ideal – old stems of perennial plants, grass cuttings, dead headed flowers, weeds and waste from vegetables that have finished cropping. Don't include any persistent weeds such as couch grass (*Elymus repens*), ground elder (*Aegopodium podagraria*) or bindweed (*Calystegia sepium*). These roots and any diseased or infected material are better burnt, otherwise they are likely to contaminate the compost and lead to problems when it is used in the garden. It is also best to avoid woody prunings, as they take too long to break down. This can be addressed by shredding this wooden material and then adding it to the compost bin. When adding grass cuttings, try to distribute them with a range of other materials, as a large quantity of grass cuttings on their own will just result in a slimy mess rather than a useful compost.

Organic waste from the kitchen can also be included, such as vegetable and fruit peelings, tea leaves and coffee grounds. Avoid adding other types of kitchen scraps as these are likely to attract rats and mice to your compost bin. Shredded newspapers, strawy horse manure, waste from pet rabbits and guinea pigs can all be added to the compost.

The best compost is created where there is a good mix of different materials and these are added in layers to the compost bin. The different layers allow air to circulate around the material and this aids the decomposition process. To speed up the process, you can add animal manure, seaweed extract or a compost activator obtained from a garden centre. These can be scattered through the compost materials. Finally, it is important to water the compost materials every so often to keep the materials damp but avoid adding too much water as this will result in a waterlogged slimy mess rather than valuable compost.

Once the material has been added, you can leave the bacteria, brandling worms and other creatures to do their work and create the compost. If you want to provide some assistance, you could turn the contents of the compost bin every so often. This simply means emptying out the container and then putting it back in again. The resultant mixing provides more oxygen for the bacteria and can help to dry out any excessively wet material.

Leaf Bins

In the autumn, it may be tempting to add fallen leaves to your compost bin. They can take a long time to break down and can result in a slimy sludge rather than compost. It is better to create a special leaf bin or cage that will enable the leaves to break down on their own and produce a valuable leaf mould for your garden. This can simply be constructed from four canes and chicken wire. Unroll the chicken wire and slowly walk around the four canes, so that the two ends meet and the four canes are enclosed. Attach the chicken netting to the canes and then fill the cage with the fallen leaves and

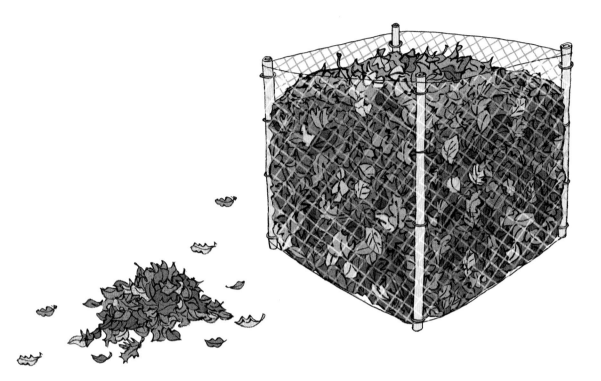

add some water. They will take around a year to decompose, but leaf mould is incredible for feeding and top dressing your plants in the spring, and can also be added to your own compost mixes.

In autumn, create a leaf bin or cage rather than adding dead leaves to a compost bin

Wormeries

In the past couple of years, wormeries have also become popular due to their ease of use and the fact they don't take up much space, particularly in a small garden. A wormery is a sealed vessel that relies solely on a working population of worms to break down the waste. A regular helping of waste is consistently required to maintain a healthy worm colony. This method of composting is ideal for urban gardening or on a balcony where space is limited. A wormery usually consists of two compartments; a lower collection sump for the liquid created and an upper composting area where the worms actively work on the waste materials. The worms used for composting are brandling, red or tiger worms. The material that can be added includes raw vegetable waste, cooked vegetables, fruit (excluding citrus peel), tea bags or leaves, eggshells, coffee grounds and small amounts of garden waste. Wormeries are usually emptied after about 8–12 months. You will need to separate the worms before using the compost, so that you can restart the wormery again. This can either be done by going through the top layer of the material and fishing them out, or alternatively in warm weather you can spread the contents out on a polythene sheet. If you then cover the centre of the compost with a wet newspaper, the worms will gravitate towards the dampness. If you use this technique, be careful to ensure that birds don't see your worms as an easy lunch.

What To Do with the Compost

Once you have a supply of brown crumbly sweet-smelling compost, you need to make good use of it in your garden. You can dig it into the top layers of your soil, but it is probably best to spread it on the top of the soil as a mulch and allow worms and other creatures to mix it into the ground. Traditionally, many gardeners viewed bare soil around their plants as garden neatness. However, bare soil loses moisture rapidly and is prone to erosion. Constantly turning over the soil can also have a damaging effect on soil fauna which are so vital in keeping the soil healthy. Alternatively, a surface mulch will conserve soil moisture, supress weeds and feed plants. Mulch also acts as a blanket layer which allows water to move through it slowly without eroding the topsoil and preventing the breakdown of the soil structure from the elements. Applying an annual mulch around March each year is ideal. Make sure your plants are not drowning in mulch as this can restrict plant growth and could result in rot. Spread the mulch evenly so that it covers any bare soil and if you do this each year, you will notice a huge improvement in plant growth and performance.

Peat-free Compost – Why Is This a Must?

If you cannot make enough compost in your own garden, then the decisions you make about the type of compost you purchase in the garden centre are important. The bogs and peatlands from which garden peat is extracted are the world's largest carbon store and provide valuable ecosystems for wildlife. When peat is harvested, CO_2 is released into the atmosphere resulting in increased global warming and climate change. In addition, peat is a raw material with a finite resource that is extremely difficult to renew as it is made from sphagnum moss that has decomposed in a unique way over thousands of years. Peat in Scottish horticulture has been used for a long time as it makes an excellent growing medium and has good ability to retain moisture. It also has the advantage that it does not become too waterlogged or saturated. However, for the benefit of the planet, your choice of compost should be limited to those that are peat free. With natural habitats being destroyed and CO_2 released into the ever-warming atmosphere, the importance of going peat free is clear. The range of these peat free alternatives is increasing all the time, but some of the most popular are made from sheep wool, bark, coconut fibres or bulrushes.

Green Manures

When you have a large area of soil and replanting it isn't possible for, say, a few months, it may be worth planting green manure cover crops that will cover the soil and feed it at the same time. These crops from the legume, grass and mustard plant families are fast growing with a high biomass and nitrogen content. They are low maintenance, and simply involve scattering the seeds over the area you want to cover. Once sown, gently rake them into the soil with a rake and keep them watered. After this, in a few weeks' time your once-bare soil will now be blanketed in productive and beneficial greenery.

Green manures grown in the summer can be managed with minimal soil disturbance. Once they have grown, allow them to die down and leave the top growth on the surface over winter. Rake off before sowing or planting the area in spring and add to the compost heap. Winter-grown green manures require deeper cultivation as you turn the roots into the soil a few months before sowing/planting an area. Any green manure will protect and aerate your topsoil structure and provide nutrients which will benefit future plants that grow in the soil. Summer-grown green manures are also good for pollinators. The most common summer green manures are: *Phacelia tanacetifolia* (fiddleneck), *Fagopyrum esculentum* (buckwheat) and *Trifolium incarnatum* (crimson clover). For winter-grown green manures sown in late summer or early autumn the most common are: *Vicia sativa* (common vetch) and *Vicia faba* (field beans), as well as winter hardy salads such as claytonia, chicory and corn salad.

Vicia sativa (common vetch), a winter-grown green manure

Compost Teas

It is also possible to create your liquid fertiliser using 'bocking 14' comfrey or nettles. The leaves of these plants are full of nitrogen, phosphorus and potassium which are all nutrients needed by growing plants. The nettles can be collected from a wild nettle patch and the 'bocking 14' comfrey can be grown in good soil with full sun. Comfrey can live for 20 or more years and, once established, needs very little maintenance. It is best to remove flowering stems in the first season to gain maximum leaf growth the following year.

The steps to creating the teas are as follows: Wearing gloves, cut off the leaves about 5cm above soil level. Fill a bucket with water and add approximately 1kg of cut or bruised leaves to around 15l of water. Press the leaves down firmly so they are covered with water and cover the container. After 4–6 weeks a noxious, (very) smelly brown liquid is ready for use. Strain the liquid and add 1 part feed to 20 parts water. Use as a summer feed for a wide range of plants in your garden or greenhouse.

Seaweed can also be used in a similar manner to create a liquid feed. Always check with local authorities before harvesting large amounts of seaweed, as you will need a licence for this. However, a small bag worth of storm washed-up seaweed can be harvested and used to make a tea, added to a compost heap or spread on vegetable beds in autumn for spring planting.

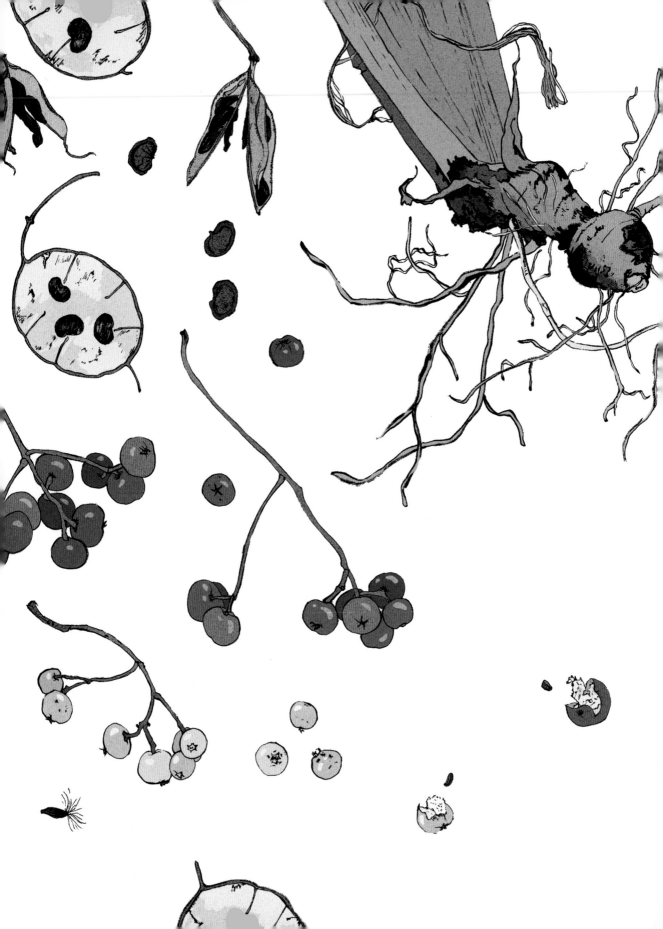

CHAPTER 12

Creating New Plants for Free – Propagation

*'Don't judge each day by the harvest you reap
but by the seeds that you plant'*
ROBERT LOUIS STEVENSON

Rather than buying new plants for your garden, you can reproduce your favourite plants for free by propagation. This can result in more plants for your own garden but can also provide stock that you can swap or share with neighbours and friends. Propagation is the reproduction of specimens of a plant by natural processes from the parent stock. In nature, plants can be reproduced from seed or vegetatively reproduced. In seed production, a plant flowers and is pollinated by insects and then sets seeds which are dispersed by various means. With pollination, the genes of both parents are carried in their offspring. The dominant gene in each seed will dictate the nature of the new plant. So, if the seed carries the genes of a tall and short plant, the new young plant can sometimes turn out tall and at other times turn out to be short. There is no guarantee that you will get the same plant each time.

With vegetative reproduction either occurring naturally or through propagation, the new plant produced is an accurate copy of the parent plant. In nature vegetative reproduction can take various forms:

Buds developing on swollen roots or tubers
    potato, dahlia, parsnip
Rhizomes – produce new plants on the end of horizontally growing underground stems
    iris, waterlily, Solomon's seal, mint

Gladiolus corm, showing how it reproduces from cormlets (small corms) which grow around the parent corm. See crocus, crocosmia and gladiolus.

Corms (bulb-like, underground swollen plant stems or stem bases, usually surrounded by papery skin) produce new plants as cormlets (small corms) that form on the top of existing corms
crocus, gladiolus

Bulbs – small auxiliary bulbs develop on the edge of existing bulbs
tulip, daffodil, snowdrop, hyacinth, bluebell, lily

Runners – send outside branches on the surface of the soil which form new plants at intervals along their length
strawberry

With all these natural vegetative reproduction forms, the gardener can lift and move the new plants being created to make room for other plants or to establish the additional plants in another part of the garden. If you have other types of plant or want to assist in the natural reproduction of plants, there are several activities that you can undertake. The most common approaches are: seed collection; layering; division; and the taking of cuttings.

Seed Collection

Seed can come in many forms such as: exploding seedheads (e.g. *Euphorbia lathyris*); capsules (e.g. poppy); berries (e.g. holly); cones (e.g. pine trees); winged seed (e.g. acer, sycamore); and catkins (e.g. birch).

Acer seeds – an example of a winged seed

You should collect the seed when it is ripe. This is often indicated by a colour change in the seedheads or capsules from green to brown, black or red. Place the picked seedheads out to dry on a greenhouse bench or a warm windowsill. If the seed is in a capsule or pod, gently crushing this when dry will tend to release the seed. If you have collected exploding seedheads, it is best to put them in a paper bag and shake them every two to three days until the ripe seeds explode into the bag.

Seed can be retrieved from berries by mashing them through a fine sieve and washing away any pulp surrounding the seed with cold water. The seed should then be left to dry for a few days.

Pine cones should be left in a warm place such as a sunny windowsill and the cone should slowly open up and seeds will fall from the cones. Nuts take a long time to germinate, but if you

score the skin of the nut with a knife and then plant in compost, you may be able to produce a new plant.

For many plants you should wait until the following autumn or spring to plant the seeds. This means good storage is required until then. For most seeds, you need to keep them dry and cool. This means placing the dry seed in labelled paper packets or envelopes within an airtight container. This should then be stored in a cool place or the refrigerator until required.

Layering

After layering a *Rhododendron*, roots develop in about 24 months

Layering involves taking one stem from a plant and putting part of it in the ground whilst leaving it attached to the parent until it develops roots. It is usually done in spring for shrubs and in early summer for climbers. The procedure involves choosing flexible young shoots on the outside of the plant that can be bent down to ground level. Then bury a length of a stem around 30cm from the tip in the soil. This last 30cm of the stem should remain exposed to the air. The stem can be held down by a forked stick or a loop of bent wire. Rooting can be encouraged by cutting a slit in the underside of the stem.

Roots should develop in around 12 months, although rhododendrons can take up to two years to root. When a good root system has formed, cut the stem from the parent plant, and transplant the new plant to its final position. You can tell when it has rooted by the more vigorous appearance of the stem. Layering is particularly suited to plants such as: *Abelia, Acer, Azalea, Camellia, Clematis, Choisya, Daphne, Forsythia, Hamamelis, Hazel, Jasminum, Magnolia, Rhododendron* and *Viburnum*.

Division

Most perennial plants can be propagated by division of their root clump and doing so every two to three years can help to maintain the health and vigour of the plant. Examples of plants that can be propagated in this way include: *Agapanthus, Anemone, Aster, Bergenia* (elephant's ears), *Convallaria* (lily-of-the-valley) *Crocosmia, Delphinium, Euphorbia, Helianthus, Hemerocallis, Hosta, Iris, Primula* (primrose), *Salvia, Sedum,* and *Verbena*.

The process involves digging up the full root clump with a fork in spring or autumn. Spring is probably the best time for more tender plants such as *Hostas*. Spring-flowering plants, such as irises, are best divided in the summer when they produce new roots. Take the root clump and shake off excess soil so that the roots are clearly visible. Then simply divide the roots into two or more pieces either by teasing them apart with your hands or levering them apart with two forks placed back-to-back in the middle of the root system. Plants with woody crowns (e.g. *Helleborus*) or fleshy roots (e.g. *Delphinium*) may require cutting with a spade. The aim is to produce clumps containing three to five healthy shoots. Cut any leaves right back to around 3cm of the roots and replant immediately or pot up in potting compost for planting later or for sharing with friends and neighbours.

Taking Cuttings

Taking cuttings is probably the most common method of propagation. There are softwood, semi-ripe, and hardwood cuttings as well as leaf cuttings. Softwood cuttings are taken in spring and early summer, from the tender new growth of the season. Semi-ripe cuttings are taken in late summer or early autumn when this year's growth has just started to go woody and hardwood cuttings are taken in mid-autumn and early winter from dormant, long straight stems. Finally, leaf cuttings only use parts of a leaf to propagate future plants.

Softwood Cuttings

Softwood cuttings are generally the quickest and most successful of all propagation techniques. They are mostly used for propagating perennials such as: *Anthemis, Aubrieta, Argyranthemum, Bidens, Cosmos, Osteospermum, Penstemon, Pelargonium, Petunia, Salvia* and *Verbena*. They can also be used for deciduous shrubs such as: *Buddleja, Fuchsia, Hydrangea, Lavatera* and *Perovskia*.

The procedure involves removing a healthy side shoot of about 5–10cm in length. Trim the shoot just below the bottom leaf joint with a very sharp knife as this is where there is a concentration of hormones to stimulate root production. Then remove the bottom leaves and leave about four leaves if they are small or two if it has large leaves such as on a geranium. Dip the cut end into a hormone rooting powder, which can be purchased from any garden centre. Then plant the cutting using a pencil or dibber in a tray or pot containing seed or cuttings compost with the first pair of leaves just above the level of the compost and water the cuttings in. Several cuttings can be put in each pot or tray. You can buy a propagator case for less than £20–£30 which consists of a tray with a transparent plastic cover that provides warmth, ventilation, and light to your cuttings. Alternatively, fasten a plastic bag over your pot or tray with an elastic band and place somewhere warm, such as a windowsill or near a radiator. Remove the bag two or three times a week to ventilate the

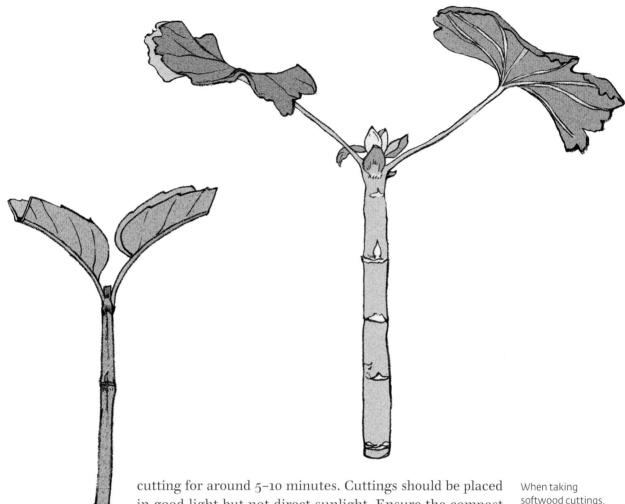

cutting for around 5–10 minutes. Cuttings should be placed in good light but not direct sunlight. Ensure the compost remains moist until the cuttings are well-rooted which takes about 2 to 3 weeks. Once the cuttings have rooted and look healthy with new leaves, harden them off for a week or two by leaving the plastic cover or bag off the cuttings and then transfer them to larger 7.5cm pots containing soilless potting compost. Once they are of a reasonable size and quite bushy, they can be planted out into the soil.

Semi-ripe Cuttings

Semi-ripe cuttings are used for evergreen herbs, conifers, box and heathers. These are very similar to softwood cuttings but involve cutting strong young shoots in their first year of growth. They should be pliable but not too soft and around

When taking softwood cuttings, trim the shoot below the bottom leaf joint. The cutting should be 5–10cm in length.

When taking hardwood cuttings, trim the top end just above a leaf joint and the bottom end just below a leaf joint. The resulting cutting should be about 20cm in length.

10–15cm in length. Trim the base of the cuttings below a leaf joint and remove leaves from the lower two-thirds of the stem. Dip the bottom of the cutting in hormone rooting powder and then insert them in a tray or pot of seed compost around 8cm apart. After watering, these types of cuttings can be put in a cold frame or out of doors covering the pot with a cut-off lemonade bottle or cloche. Try to avoid direct sunlight – they should get enough light for photosynthesis but not so much sunlight that would make them wilt. The cuttings should root in around 6–8 weeks and can then be individually potted.

Hardwood Cuttings

Hardwood cuttings are generally taken when the plant is dormant after leaf fall and avoiding periods of severe frost. It is suitable for most deciduous shrubs and climbers including: *Abelia*, *Buddleja*, *Cornus* (dogwood), *Forsythia*, *Jasminum*, *Lonicera* (honeysuckle), *Philadelphus* (mock orange), *Ribes* (flowering currant), *Rosa* (rose), and *Viburnums*. It is also suitable for fruit bushes such as gooseberries; black, red and white currants; and trees such as *Populus* (poplars) and *Salix* (willow). Although usually restricted to deciduous plants, some evergreen cuttings such as *Cotoneaster*, *Ilex* (holly), *Ligustrum* (privet) and *Skimmia* can be taken in the same way.

For any of these, simply cut around 25cm lengths of shoot from the current season's wood in the late autumn. Trim the top end to just above a leaf joint and the bottom to just below a leaf joint – this should result in a stem of around 20cm. Dip the bottom in hormone rooting powder and plant the cuttings firmly into garden soil with around 8cm showing above the surface. If the soil has a lot of clay, it is best to put some sharp sand at the bottom of a small v-shaped slit trench before digging the cuttings in and watering well. Hardwood cuttings are generally slow to root but by the following autumn, each cutting should have a good root system. They should then be planted around 15–25cm apart in rows and by the following year, they should be able to be moved to their final permanent positions.

Leaf Cuttings

Leaf cuttings are used for plants that don't have any stems such as *Streptocarpus*, *Saintpaulia* (African violet) and *Begonia Rex*. As the name suggests, the technique involves cutting off a healthy green leaf from the parent plant. Taking care to remember which is the top and the bottom of the leaf, slice across the leaf to create sections approximately 3cm wide. Insert the cut sections into seed or cuttings compost with the part of the leaf that was nearest the parent plant being pushed into the compost with approximately 2cm remaining above the surface. The resulting tray or pot will look as if you have a number of mini gravestones sticking up out of the soil. Keep the cuttings warm and watered and they can be potted on when a new young plant is produced at the bottom of each cutting.

Leaf cuttings are made from plants which have no stems. The cutting should be placed in the compost pointing in the same the direction that it was growing on the parent plant. Plantlets with roots will form at the bottom of each cutting.

Alternative Sources of Plants

There will be times when you will want new plants for your garden and therefore cuttings will not be possible. There are many inexpensive sources of plants. You can obtain cuttings or divided plants from your neighbours or friends, or you can arrange to swap different plants with them. Local gardening clubs and allotments often sell off plants for fund-raising purposes, and these can be much cheaper than buying from commercial garden centres. You may even want to suggest to your local school that they have a plant sale where parents donate plants and these are sold to raise money for the school. Finally, DIY stores, supermarkets and garden centres may also discount plants that don't look at their best, however, with a little loving care, many of these plants can be coaxed back to full health. Nature has a way of surviving if it is given the opportunity.

Collecting and Buying Native Plants

It is against the law to dig up plants in the wild without first asking permission of the landowner. There is also a list of protected species that it is illegal to pick, dig up, damage or sell. There are also certain areas of high nature conservation interest, including nature reserves, and areas of special scientific interest in which all plants are protected by law. It is therefore more prudent to start plants from seed or to purchase plants from a specialist nursery. An extensive list of nurseries is provided near the end of this book.

CHAPTER 13

Attracting Specific Species with Planting

'One should pay attention to even the smallest crawling creature for these too may have a valuable lesson to teach us'
BLACK ELK

The next few pages set out some of the key birds, bees, butterflies, other insects, aquatic species and night life that we can enjoy in our gardens and the best plants to attract them. There are, of course, many other creatures required to create a healthy ecosystem, but creating a full listing of their preferred habitat and food sources goes beyond what is possible in a book of this type. So, what we have here are some of the more popular creatures that can enhance a British garden.

Attracting Birds

Garden birds in the UK can be categorised into four groupings. These are omnivores, seed-eaters, insect-feeders, and fruit-eaters.

Omnivores

Omnivores feed on a wide range of different foods, which means there is usually sufficient in a garden whatever time of year. They include the blue tit, which eats insects and seeds; the sparrow which eats insects, seeds, and buds; the chaffinch which eats seeds, caterpillars, and spiders; the blackbird which eats earthworms, insects and fruit; and the robin which likes insects, fruit, worms and snails. Other members of this group include jays, magpies and jackdaws which eat seeds, fruit, slugs, spiders, smaller birds' eggs and carrion.

The omnivorous blue tit

PLANTS TO ATTRACT OMNIVORES

Crataegus monogyna (hawthorn) provides buds, nectar, fruit, and insects

Rubus fruticosus (bramble) provides buds, nectar, fruit and insects and spiders as well as ground cover protection for nesting birds

Hedera helix (ivy) provides insects, caterpillars and spiders plus nectar, fruit, and shelter

Seed-eaters

A number of garden birds rely solely on seeds for their diet, the most common are the goldfinch, tree sparrow, brambling, greenfinch and crossbill. Others such as the siskin, linnet, dunnock, redpoll, nuthatch, great tit and reed bunting combine seeds with insects in their diet, particularly when seeds are less available in spring and early summer. All of these birds are a common sight on bird tables in the winter.

The seed-eating goldfinch

PLANTS TO ATTRACT SEED-EATERS

Dipsacus fullonum (teasel)
Panicum miliaceum (millet)
Silybum marianum (milk thistle)
Helianthus annuus (sunflower)
Taraxacum officinale (dandelion)
Onopordum acanthium (cotton thistle)

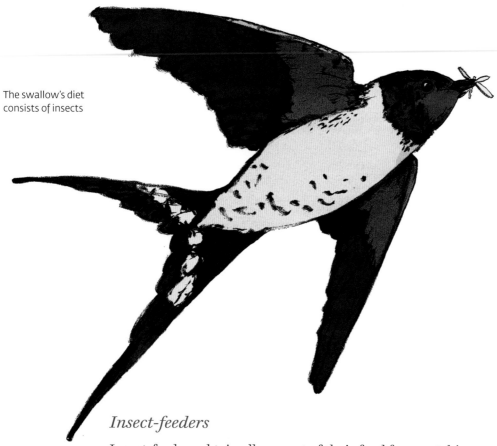

The swallow's diet consists of insects

Insect-feeders

Insect-feeders obtain all or most of their food from catching insects on the wing (swallows, swifts, house martins and fly catchers), by digging into trees (woodpeckers), or by collecting insects from plants (wrens, goldcrests and chiffchaffs). Planting insect-attracting plants will result in more insect-feeding birds appearing. A wildflower meadow or a pond will provide an insect-rich food source for these birds. These birds are rarely seen on bird tables unless the winter is particularly severe.

PLANTS TO ATTRACT INSECT-FEEDERS

Achillea millefolium (yarrow)
Angelica archangelica (angelica)
Lavandula angustifolia (English lavender)
Lunaria annua (honesty)
Melissa officinalis (lemon balm)
Prunus padus (bird cherry)

Fruit-eaters

Fruit-eating birds include the redwing and garden warbler, which eat only fruit, and fieldfares, mistle thrushes and blackcaps, which have fruit as a key part of their diet but may also eat insects or seeds. Several of the omnivorous birds, such as the blackbird, will also eat fruit when it is available, but are happy to seek out other food when the fruit season is over. Windfall apples or growing plants that produce berries, such as rowan trees, fruiting viburnums and holly, will attract these birds. They are particularly attracted to the colour red, so red and red–orange berries are always eaten first, with white or yellow ones being left until later in the winter.

The fruit-eating redwing

PLANTS TO ATTRACT FRUIT-EATERS

Cotoneaster horizontalis (herringbone cotoneaster)
Euonymus europaeus (spindle)
Ilex aquifolium (holly)
Lonicera periclymenum (honeysuckle)
Sambucus nigra (elder)
Sorbus aucuparia (rowan)
Viburnum opulus (guelder rose)

Attracting Bees and Other Insects

Honeybees (left) and bumblebees (opposite) are major pollinators

Many insects will take up residence in your garden. This section will focus on attracting five key species that are particularly valuable to the wildlife garden. These are honeybees, bumblebees, hoverflies, ladybirds and butterflies.

Honeybees

Honeybees live in organised colonies or hives. Some colonies of wild bees live in hollow trees or cavities in walls, as well as those in hives kept by beekeepers for the production of honey. Honeybees are major pollinators of wildflowers and fruit trees. At the end of the summer, honey is stored for winter food during hibernation.

PLANTS TO ATTRACT HONEYBEES

Calluna vulgaris (heather)
Satureja montana (winter savory)
Malus domestica (apple)
Prunus domestica (plum)
Thymus vulgaris (thyme)
Rosmarinus officinalis (rosemary)
Tilia cordata (lime)
Trifolium repens (white clover)

Bumblebees

Bumblebees are large, hairy bees, generally black with varying degrees of yellow banding. The most common bumblebees include garden, buff-tailed, red-tailed, white-tailed and field bumblebees. They are social insects and live in colonies of up to 200 workers. The bees do not survive the winter, leaving only the young queens hibernating underground to form new colonies in the spring. They are important pollinators of many plants and fruiting trees.

PLANTS TO ATTRACT BUMBLEBEES

Antirrhinum majus (snapdragon)
Digitalis purpurea (foxglove)
Lamium maculatum (white deadnettle)
Lonicera periclymenum (honeysuckle)
Papaver rhoeas (corn poppy)
Trifolium pratense (red clover)

Hoverflies

Although these brightly-coloured insects look like bees or wasps, they are in fact true flies and do not sting. There are about 250 different hoverfly species in Britain. Most of the species are mimics and take on the colouring of wasps, honey- or bumblebees to provide a defence from predators. They are very useful insects to attract into the garden because their larvae feed on aphids, some managing to consume up to 500 aphids a week. They are also useful pollinators, favouring flowers with exposed pollen and nectar, such as plants of the carrot and daisy families.

PLANTS TO ATTRACT HOVERFLIES

CaIendula officinalis (marigold)
Clematis vitalba (old man's beard)
Foeniculum vulgare (fennel)
Hedera helix (ivy)
Levisticum officinale (lovage)
Tagetes patula (French marigold)

Ladybirds

Ladybirds are a type of beetle that are easy to recognise. The most familiar have bright red wing cases with black spots, while others are black and yellow, white and brown, or even striped. The commonest species are the two-spot and larger seven-spot ladybirds, although about 40 others can also be found in the UK. Their bright colour warns predators that they are poisonous and should be left alone. They are important for gardeners because all ladybirds are voracious aphid eaters, as are their larvae. Ladybirds lay their eggs on aphid-infested plants so that when the larvae emerge there is ample food for them. The adults hibernate in cracks in wood and bark, often grouping in their hundreds to keep warm.

Ladybirds and their larvae are voracious aphid eaters

PLANTS TO ATTRACT LADYBIRDS

Rosa species (roses)
Urtica dioica (stinging nettle)
Trifolium pratense (red clover)

Butterflies

Small tortoiseshell (top right), red admiral (bottom left) and peacock butterflies (opposite)

Butterflies are some of the most beautiful insect visitors to our gardens. One of the commonest garden butterflies throughout the UK is the small tortoiseshell. It can be identified by its bright orange and black colouring with a row of blue crescents around the wing edges. Underneath, they are camouflaged dark grey and brown. The females tend to lay their eggs on tender, young stinging nettles in batches. Caterpillars hatch after about 10 days and spin a web over the plant's growing tip. Caterpillars are bristly and black with two discontinuous yellow lines along their sides. Adults often hibernate in houses, outbuildings and sheds. Other garden visitors include the red admiral, painted lady, peacock and the common blue. The large white is also common throughout the UK, however, it is frequently disliked by gardeners as the caterpillars can severely damage brassica crops such as cabbage, kale, and Brussels sprouts.

The red admiral has dark black-brown wings, each with an orange-red band. The forewing tips are black with white spots; the underside is orange, blue and white, while the hindwings are dark brown. During the summer, females lay single eggs on the growing tips of nettles. Caterpillars are bristly and dark with a pale yellow stripe running down each side. The caterpillars live within a tent formed by folding and fastening the edges of a leaf together with silk.

The painted lady has a pale buffy orange background colour to the upper wings. The forewings have black tips marked with white spots; the hindwings have rows of black spots. The undersides are pale with blue eyespots. Painted ladies do not hibernate in the UK; instead they migrate to and from north Africa. They tend to arrive in

late May and June. Females lay
their small, green eggs on plants
such as nettles and thistles.
Caterpillars are black, speckled with tiny white spots and have
a yellow stripe down each side. The caterpillars hatch, eat the
underside of the leaf, and construct a tent of folded leaves
fastened with silk.

The peacock butterfly has brownish-red wings, each with
a single, large peacock-feather-like eyespot. It also has a
black, well-camouflaged underside. It is very common in
England and Wales but less so in Scotland. It lays eggs in
batches up to 400–500 and the caterpillars, which are black
speckled with white spots, spin a communal web in which
they live and feed. The adults hibernate during winter in dark
crevices and sheds and tree holes.

Male common blues have violet-blue upper wings with
grey-beige undersides and the females tend to have brown
upper wings and orange crescents. The caterpillars are short,
green and furry. They feed on the underside of young leaves
creating silvery blotches on the leaves. The adults drink
nectar from flat-headed flowers. Creating a wildflower
meadow with clovers and vetches will encourage these
butterflies.

Large white butterflies have white wings with broad black
tips on the forewings. Females also have two black spots and
a black streak on each wing. Females lay clusters of 50–100
yellowish eggs on the undersides of leaves. The caterpillars
are grey-green mottled with black spots and yellow stripes.
The caterpillars feed communally, making large holes in a
plant's leaves, and the adults drink nectar from flowers.

PLANTS TO ATTRACT BUTTERFLIES

For small tortoiseshell, red admiral, painted lady, peacock:

Hebe salicifolia (shrubby veronica)
Origanum vulgare (marjoram)
Sedum spectabile (ice plant)
Aster novi-belgii (Michaelmas daisy)
Buddleja davidii (butterfly bush)
Centranthus ruber (red valerian)

FOR COMMON BLUE:

Hedera helix (ivy)
Origanum vulgare (majoram)
Lavandula angustifolia (English lavender)
Mentha spicata (spearmint)
Rubus fruticosus (bramble)
Thymus vulgaris (thyme)

FOR LARGE WHITE:

Centranthus ruber (red valerian)
Erysimum cheiri (wallflower)
Hesperis matronalis (sweet rocket)
Lunaria annua (honesty)
Myosotis arvensis (forget-me-not)

Large white (top),
painted lady (middle)
and common blue
(bottom) butterflies

Pond Life

Ponds and water features in a garden can attract a wide range of amphibians and insects. The most common are frogs, toads, newts, dragonflies and damselflies.

Frogs and Toads

Frogs and toads need water for breeding and for the first stages of life as tadpoles. During the winter, they hibernate under rotting leaves stones or logs near their breeding sites. In the spring, they migrate back to a pond where they will mate and produce eggs in the form of frog spawn or toad spawn.

The most frequent visitors to gardens are the common frog and the common toad. The common frog has smooth skin that varies in colour from grey, olive green and yellow to brown in irregular dark blotches. They also have a dark stripe around their eyes and eardrum, and dark bars on their legs. Common frogs are most active at night, they eat insects, snails, slugs and worms. Their tadpoles feed on algae but may become carnivorous.

The common frog – a frequent visitor to gardens with ponds and other water features

Common toads have broad, squat, warty bodies that vary from dark brown, grey and olive-green to sandy coloured. Toads tend to be solitary and live away from water under logs or vegetation during the day, emerging in the evening to feed on insect larvae, spiders, slugs and worms. Larger toads may also take slow worms and harvest mice. Unlike frogs, they tend to walk rather than hop. They can also live up to around 10–12 years.

Although frogs and toads don't tend to eat vegetation once fully grown, they seek certain types of aquatic plant to provide protective cover for eggs, tadpoles and the adults.

PLANTS TO ATTRACT FROGS AND TOADS

Butomus umbellatus (flowering rush)
Nymphaea alba (white water lily)
Iris pseudacorus (yellow flag)
Mentha aquatica (water mint)

Mentha aquatica
(water mint)

Newts

Smooth newts, or common newts, are olive-green or pale-brown with a bright orange, black-spotted underside. In the breeding season, males develop a wavy crest from their heads to their tails. They are nocturnal and spend the day hiding under large stones or compost heaps. They lay their eggs on submerged broadleaved aquatic plants. The eggs hatch into tadpoles and over a period of around 10 weeks they change into juvenile newts. They eat insects, slugs, worms, tadpoles, water snails and small crustaceans.

The smooth newt lays its eggs on submerged broadleaved aquatic plants

PLANTS TO ATTRACT NEWTS

Ceratophyllum demersum (hornwort)
Marsilea quadrifolia (European water clover)
Ranunculus aquatilis (common water crowfoot)
Aponogeton distachyos (water hyacinth)
Callitriche palustris (water starwort)
Hydrocharis morsus-ranae (frogbit)

Dragonflies and Damselflies

Other inhabitants of garden ponds are the dragonfly and damselfly. They vary in colouring, but can be extremely vibrant shades of blue, red, and green. Dragonflies are chunkier with short bodies, whereas damsels are the opposite and have extremely long and narrow bodies. Damselflies rest with their wings closed, and dragonflies spread theirs like an aeroplane. They all lay their eggs just below the surface of a pond. The eggs hatch out as nymphs, spending two to five years in the pond before climbing out up the leaves or stem of a water plant to shed their skin and emerge in their adult form. The adults feed on midges and other small insects by swooping over the water to catch them in flight.

PLANTS TO ATTRACT DRAGONFLIES AND DAMSELFLIES

Iris pseudacorus (yellow flag)
Lythrum salicaria (purple loosestrife)
Nymphaea alba (white waterlily)

Dragonflies (left) and damselflies (right) lay their eggs just below the surface of the water

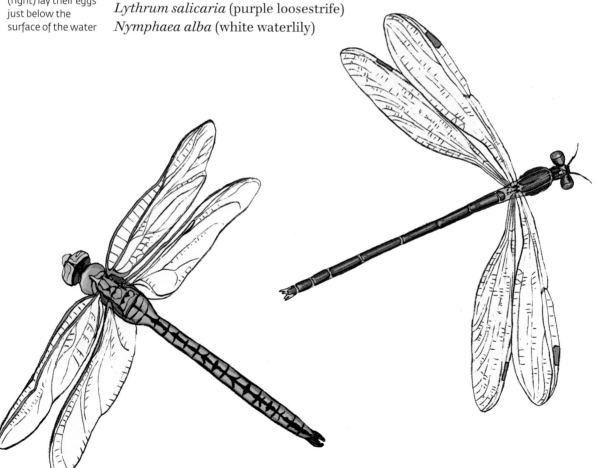

Nightlife

Many creatures, including stag beetles, millipedes, slugs, snails, woodlice, wood mice, dormice and earthworms emerge at night when it is cooler, and the darkness makes them less obvious to their predators. Owls, hedgehogs, and badgers, which feed on these creatures, have also adapted to a nocturnal way of life.

Similarly, moths rest during the day and start flying to nectar in the evening. Moths are related to butterflies and share a similar life cycle. In Britain there are around 2,500 species of moth, and the adults and the caterpillars are an important food source for birds, bats, and other mammals. The more moths you can attract to your garden, the greater the likelihood of attracting bats.

Adult moths are important pollinators of flowers and some trees. There are a number of plants that have flowers which open at the end of the day and stay open into the night. Many of them are scented to attract moths. They also tend to be white, cream, yellow or pale pink as moths are attracted by white or light-coloured flowers, which tend to glow in the pale evening light.

PLANTS FOR ATTRACTING MOTHS

Centranthus ruber (red valerian)
Hesperis matronalis (sweet rocket)
Jasminum officinale (jasmine)
Lonicera periclymenum (honeysuckle)
Malus sylvestris (crab apple)
Matthiola longipetala subsp. *bicornis* (night-scented stock)
Nicotiana alata (tobacco plant)
Oenothera biennis (evening primrose)
Pinus sylvestris (Scots pine)
Prunus spinosa (sloe)
Saponaria officinalis (soapwort)
Silene vulgaris (bladder campion)

List of
Specialist Nurseries

Abi & Tom's Garden Plants
Halecat, Witherslack, Cumbria LA11 6RT
015395 52946
www.abiandtom.co.uk
Trees, shrubs, herbaceous perennials, alpines

Alba Trees
Lower Winton, Gladsmuir, East Lothian EH33 2AL
01620 825 058
www.albatrees.co.uk
Trees

Arvensis Perennials
Lower Wraxall, Bradford-on-Avon, Wiltshire BA15 2RU
01225 867761
www.arvensisperennials.co.uk
Herbaceous perennials

Ashwood Nurseries
Ashwood Lower Lane, Kingswinford, West Midlands DY6 0AE
01384 401996
www.ashwoodnurseries.com
Trees, shrubs, herbaceous perennials, alpines

Barcham Trees Plc
Eye Hill Drove, Ely, Cambridgeshire CB7 5XF
01353 720950
www.barcham.co.uk
Trees

Beth Chatto Nursery
Beth Chatto Gardens Ltd, Elmstead Market, Colchester,
Essex CO7 7DB
01206 822 007
www.bethchatto.co.uk
Herbaceous perennials

Binny Plants
Binny Estate, Ecclesmachan Road, Uphall, West Lothian EH52 6NL
07753 626117
www.binnyplants.com
Herbaceous perennials, shrubs and show peonies

Bluebell Cottage Nursery
Bluebell Cottage, Lodge Lane, Dutton, near Warrington,
Cheshire WA4 4HP
01928 713718
www.bluebellcottage.co.uk
Herbaceous perennials

British Wildflower Seeds
Hookgate Cottage, South Brewham, Somerset BA10 0LQ
01749 812355
www.britishwildflowermeadowseeds.co.uk
British wildflowers

Burncoose Nurseries
Gwennap, Redruth, Cornwall TR16 6BJ
01209 860316
www.burncoose.co.uk
Trees, shrubs, herbaceous perennials

Claire Austin Hardy Plants
White Hopton Farm, Wern Lane, Sarn, Newtown, Powys SY16 4EN
0168 667 0342
www.claireaustin-hardyplants.co.uk
Herbaceous perennials

Claremont Aquatic Nurseries
Cocker Bar Road, Leyland, Lancashire PR26 7TA
01772 421860
www.claremontaquatic.co.uk
Aquatic plants

Cotswold Garden Flowers
Sands Lane, Badsey, Evesham, Worcestershire WR11 7EZ
01386 422829
www.cotswoldgardenflowers.co.uk
Herbaceous perennials

Crocus
Nursery Court, London Road, Windlesham, Surrey GU20 6LQ
01344 578000
www.crocus.co.uk
Trees, Shrubs, Herbaceous Perennials

David Austin
David Austin Roses, Bowling Green Lane, Albrighton,
Shropshire WV7 3HB
0800 111 4699
www.davidaustinroses.co.uk/
Roses

East Neuk Perennials
Smithy Cottage, Balchrystie, Colinsburgh, Fife KY9 1HE
07984 302241
www.eastneukperennials.co.uk
Herbaceous perennials

Frank P. Matthews Ltd
Berrington Court, Tenbury Wells, Worcestershire WR15 8TH
01584 810214
www.frankpmatthews.com
Trees

Glendoick
Glencarse, Perthshire, Scotland PH2 7NS
01738 860260
www.glendoick.com
Trees, shrubs, herbaceous perennials, Rhododendron specialists

Great Dixter Nursery
Great Dixter House & Gardens, Northiam, Rye,
East Sussex TN31 6PH
01797 254044
www.greatdixter.co.uk
Herbaceous perennials

Hardy's Cottage Garden Plants
Priory Lane Nursery, Freefolk Priors, Whitchurch,
Hampshire RG28 7FA
01256 896533
www.hardysplants.co.uk
Herbaceous perennials

Hayloft Nursery
Hayloft Plants, The Pack House, Manor Farm Nursery, Pensham,
Pershore WR10 3HB
01386 562999
www.hayloft.co.uk
Rare and unusual trees, shrubs, herbaceous perennials, bulbs

Macplants

Berrybank Nursery, 5 Boggs Holdings, Pencaitland,
East Lothian EH34 5BA
01875 341179
www.macplants.co.uk
Alpines, herbaceous perennials and grasses

Pictorial Meadows

Manor Oaks Farmhouse, 389 Manor Lane, Sheffield S2 1UL
0114 267 7635
www.pictorialmeadows.co.uk
Meadow seed and turf

Plants for Ponds (online only)

01920 823322
www.plantsforponds.co.uk
Aquatic plants

R & B Nursery Ltd

Dryden Walled Garden, Roslin, Midlothian EH25 9SX
0131 663 1944
www.rbnursery.co.uk
Trees

Sarah Raven

Perch Hill Farm, Willingford Lane, Brightling, Robertsbridge,
East Sussex TN32 5HP
0345 092 0283
www.sarahraven.com
Shrubs, herbaceous perennials, bulbs

Scotia Seeds (online only)

Mavisbank, Farnell, Brechin, Angus DD9 6TR
01356 626425
www.scotiaseeds.co.uk
Native (Scottish) wildflower seed

Special Plants Nursery

Greenways Lane, Cold Ashton, Wiltshire SN14 8LA
01225 891686
www.specialplants.net
Herbaceous perennials

Waterside Nursery (online only)

07931 557082
www.watersidenursery.co.uk
Aquatic plants

Glossary

Annual A plant that completes its full life cycle in a single growing season

Bat box An artificial roost designed to encourage bats into areas where there are few roosting sites

Biennial A biennial plant takes two years to complete its biological life cycle with the plant only flowering in its second year

Biological controls A method of controlling pests such as insects using other organisms

Bird box A box for wild birds to nest

Bird feeder A container filled with seed or nuts aimed at attracting wild birds

Bog plant A semi-aquatic plant that grows in soft wet soil

Bumblebee pot An artificial nest for bumblebees consisting of a small terracotta pot filled with dry leaves, straw, wool, grass or moss

Bughouse An artificial nesting site for insects and small mammals consisting of wood, straw and tiles. Often made using wooden pallets

Bulb An underground storage organ of a plant (such as the lily, onion, hyacinth, or tulip) that is usually formed underground and made up of layered fleshy scales that are modified leaves

Camera trap A camera that is automatically triggered by the presence of an animal or bird

Companion planting The close planting of different plants that protect each other from pests

Compost Decayed organic material used as a fertiliser for growing plants

Compost tea A concentrated organic liquid fertiliser that is made from steeping compost material such as nettles in water

Coppice belt A grove of small trees or shrubs maintained by periodic cutting or pruning to encourage greater biodiversity for wildlife by having multiple stems rather than individual tree trunks

Corm An underground stem base such as a crocus that is internally structured with solid tissues that distinguish them from a bulb, which is mostly made up of layered fleshy scales

Cutting A piece of the stem or root of a plant that is used in horticulture for propagation

Dead hedge A barrier constructed from cut branches, saplings and foliage

Defensive barrier A method of protecting plants, particularly fruit and vegetables, from birds, rabbits, slugs and snails

Division A form of plant propagation in which new plants are propagated by separating material from the parent plant

Flowering lawn A lawn that incorporates some wildflowers planted into it

Green manure A crop (such as clover) which is dug into the soil while green to enrich the soil

Hardwood cutting A cutting taken from the mature wood of a deciduous shrub, fruit bush or tree

Hedgehog home An artificial nest designed to encourage hedgehogs

Layering A form of propagation that encourages new plants to form roots while still attached to the parent plant

Leaf cutting A form of propagation using only a leaf or a part of a leaf

Marginal plant Plants that grow around the damp margins or shallow water at the edge of a pond

Mulch A covering of material placed on the surface of soil to supress weeds, retain moisture and improve soil organic matter

Mycorrhizal fungus Beneficial fungi growing in association with plant roots that provide moisture and nutrients to the plant from the soil through fungal strands.

Native plant A plant that has naturally developed in a particular region or ecosystem

Nectar Border A border that offers sustenance to a wide range of pollinators

Nematode A microscopic worm that can be used to control pests such as aphids and slugs

Non-native plant A plant that does not naturally occur in a particular region or ecosystem

Oxygenator plant A plant which helps to maintain the oxygen level in pond water

Perennial A plant that lives for several years

Propagation The breeding of new plants

Rain garden An area of vegetation that catches rainwater and then releases it very slowly, which helps reduce the severity and likelihood of flooding

Resin-bonded gravel path A form of path created by scattering loose dried aggregates onto a coating of resin creating a solid surface that lets water drain through

Rhizome A continuously growing horizontal underground stem which puts out lateral shoots and roots at intervals

Runners Slender stems that grow horizontally along the ground, giving rise to roots at points called nodes

Semi-ripe cutting A type of softwood cutting taken toward the end of the growing season

Softwood cutting A piece of plant stem taken from a woody shrub or bush during the growing season

Soil type Categories of soil such as sand, silt or clay

Tree stake A wooden post used to anchor, support, and protect a recently planted tree

Vegetative reproduction A form of reproduction where the new plant grows from the leaves, stem or roots of the original plant

Wild fence A fence with climbers growing on it
Wildflower meadow An area of perennial meadow plants
Wildlife hedge A hedge grown to attract wildlife
Woodland glade An area of underplanting below a tree canopy

Index